The Love
of Friends

The Love of Friends

A Celebration of Women's Friendships

Barbara Alpert

BERKLEY BOOKS, NEW YORK

This book is an original publication of The Berkley Publishing Group.

THE LOVE OF FRIENDS

A Berkley Book / published by arrangement with
the author

PRINTING HISTORY
Berkley trade paperback edition / December 1997

The Putnam Berkley World Wide Web site address is
http://www.berkley.com

ISBN: 0-425-16058-0

BERKLEY®
Berkley Books are published by
The Berkley Publishing Group, a member of Penguin Putnam Inc.,
200 Madison Avenue, New York, New York 10016.
BERKLEY and the "B" design
are trademarks belonging to Berkley Publishing Corporation.

PRINTED IN THE UNITED STATES OF AMERICA

10 9 8 7 6 5 4 3 2 1

For my women friends everywhere who fill my life with joy, and in memory of Susan, who reminded me how precious life is.

Introduction

They are the family we choose to surround us, the sisters bound by love instead of blood. They know when we are lonely, and appear without being called. When we feel lost, they provide a living map to what comes next; when we doubt everything about ourselves, they remind us who we are.

Our women friends are the richest treasure we possess, and the importance of friendship in women's lives cannot be overemphasized. These precious, powerful relationships sustain us when everything else seems in flux; if we're lucky, our friendships may endure for decades and across thousands of miles.

I cherish the close relationships I've had with women friends for as long as I can remember. So many of my best memories are inextricably linked to the girls and women who shared them: classmates in school and cabinmates in camp; the college roommate who always made me smile in the dark; the travel companions who added to my pleasure in new places and exotic destinations.

Because I've always loved the feeling of sisterhood I got from reading and hearing about other women's friendships, I decided to gather stories, letters, and remembrances of women from all walks of life into a volume that would celebrate these intimate, loving, often inspiring "sisters under the skin." Listening to all these women talk and write about their dearest friends gave me such pleasure—and persuaded me that true friendship is not only a gift but a responsibility, a commitment. Friendships take time and caring to sustain; more than that, they flourish only when friends recognize and celebrate the many facets of the women they love.

As I started talking to women about their friendships, and throughout my research, I would scribble notes to myself. One scrawl read, "A friendship is exactly like a marriage, with a vow, spoken or simply understood, to love and honor each other in soul and spirit, to stick by one another through thick and thin." In a very real sense, true friends commit to those they love for richer and for poorer, in sickness and in health. No license is signed, no ceremony witnessed, but the bonds of friendship are so often stronger than those which join a man and woman together.

Still, even the closest friendships, no matter how strong, will be tested—by absence and by anger, by illness and by age. And the friends to whom we've given our hearts over the years often need more: they need our courage and endurance. Sometimes, they need to know we won't leave.

I learned firsthand over the past year how a close friendship can be tested, and how difficult it is sometimes to care for someone you love. When my friend Susan was diagnosed with cancer, I did whatever I could: feeding the cat, visiting her in the hospital and at home, helping her find places to store her car or get her laundry done. I felt needed as I have rarely felt in my life, sitting next to her during chemo treatments and bringing over Chinese food so I could be sure she was eating. I wanted her to get well, but if that wasn't possible, I wanted to help her live the rest of her life the best she could. Toward the end, she sometimes vented her anger at me, which did hurt. But I promised her that no matter what, she could always call me and I'd come. (One night the phone did ring at 4 A.M. . . . !)

I still find myself saving cartoons from *The New Yorker* I know would make her smile. She is alive in my memory, and I can't enter a thrift shop without thinking of her. Bebe Moore Campbell once wrote that sometimes friendship outlives our friends, that we carry with us the gifts of a friendship even once a beloved friend is gone. I know that it's true.

Gathering together the pieces that fill this volume reminded me daily that the women who keep our secrets and support our dreams are so important, we must make time to cherish them. If this book encourages you to call up a childhood friend you haven't seen in years, or inspires you to write a letter to a pal you've lately taken for granted, I'll be very satisfied. I hope you'll agree that *The Love of Friends* provides a gift to treasure, a keepsake of times when women put their hearts on paper, shared poignant tales of tenderness, or simply made each other laugh.

—Barbara Alpert

From quiet homes and first beginning,
Out to the undiscovered ends,
There's nothing worth the wear of winning,
But laughter and the love of friends.

—Hilaire Belloc, *Dedicatory Ode*

The taxi that I took at Orly drove me past the Cathedral of Notre Dame to the hotel where I had told my friend I would meet her. As we crossed the bridge in front of the cathedral I saw her, walking in her blue coat. (I had helped her choose the coat; she was afraid it made her look short-waisted.) She was carrying red peonies. I am sure I must have seen flowers like that before: full-throated, vivid, held against dark-blue wool. But they were a miracle to me, those flowers. I called my friend's name out the taxi window. The taxi stopped. She got into it, her arms full of flowers. She had bought them for me, she said, because they reminded her of me. If you were a flower, she said, you'd be a dark-red peony.

—*Mary Gordon, novelist*

Each New Year's Eve of my life has brought back the memory of that night. Julia and I lay in twin beds and she recited odds and ends of poetry—every once in a while she would stop and ask me to recite, but I didn't know anything—Dante in Italian, Heine in German, and even though I could not understand either language, the sounds were so lovely that I felt a sweet sadness as if much was ahead in the world, much that was going to be fine and fulfilling if I could ever find my way. I did recite Mother Goose and she did Donne's "Julia," and laughed with pleasure "at his tribute to me." I was ashamed to ask if it was a joke.

Very late she turned her head away for sleep, but I said, "More, Julia, please. Do you know more?" And she turned on the light again and recited from Ovid and Catullus, names to me without countries.

I don't know when I stopped listening to look at the lovely face propped against the pillow—the lamp throwing fine lights on the thick dark hair. I cannot say now that I knew or had ever used the words gentle or delicate or strong, but I did think that night that it was the most beautiful face I had ever seen.

—*Lillian Hellman remembering her friend Julia*

Idgie, who was barefoot, started walking over to the big oak tree and about halfway there, turned to see if Ruth was watching. When she got about ten feet from the tree, she made sure again that Ruth was still watching. Then she did the most amazing thing. She very slowly tiptoed up to it, humming very softly, and stuck her hand with the jar in it, in the hole in the middle of the oak.

All of a sudden, Ruth heard a sound like a buzz saw, and the sky went black as hordes of angry bees swarmed out of the hole.

In seconds, Idgie was covered from head to foot with thousands of bees. Idgie just stood there, and in a minute, carefully pulled her hand out of the tree and started walking slowly back toward Ruth, still humming. By the time she had gotten back, almost all the bees had flown away, and what had been a completely black figure was now Idgie, standing there, grinning from ear to ear, with a jar of wild honey.

She held it up, offering the jar to Ruth. "Here you are, madame, this is for you."

> —*from* Fried Green Tomatoes at the Whistle Stop Cafe *by*
> Fannie Flagg

I want my friends to stretch me intellectually, to understand my longings and dreams and encourage me to embrace the future in life-enhancing ways. In bad times I want us to be there for each other physically and spiritually . . .

I think of close friends as soul mates—friends we love and trust so implicitly that we want to think out loud with them. Listening and talking, communicating and sharing silences—these are the main events. What I'm most attracted to in my friends are their spirits: They are people who love life, who are passionate, who take risks to live fully, who are sensitive to feelings and idiosyncrasies, who share this goodness with me. Having and being a friend means wanting only the best for one another, and the bond allows each friend to grow and flower to [her] fullest capacity. A friendship can grow as far as you will allow it. When we have a friend who encourages us to be ourselves, who loves us as we are, we have an incomparable treasure.

—*Alexandra Stoddard*

I do, indeed, adopt you, dearest Mrs. Hoare, as a "friend upon paper"—a true and dear friend! My best and most congenial habits of association and intercourse have so begun; and I do not think I have ever lost one, who has so taken to me and to whom I have so taken. . . .

I live quite alone, having no relations—almost literally none, except a few distant relations too grand to claim. Many kind friends I have—some of them persons of note in literature; but I think I prefer those who love letters without actually following the trade of authorship. . . .

> —*Mary Russell Mitford, nineteenth-century author and passionate gardener, in a letter to her new friend Mrs. Hoare, Spring 1853*

[She] was one of the those young women that you meet and know absolutely nothing's going to stop. She had enormous energy and vitality, in this sort of brute sense. She's always about twice as smart as everyone else in the room. Once she moved to L.A., she was four times as smart. She's smarter than everyone else, and yet she has these areas I can only regard as mystifying. Like her New Age garbage and crystal gazing and things like that. But I forgive her.

We both look forward to the day when we can stop the van and say, "Antique store, 20-minute break!" But we've never gotten to that moment in the movie business.

> —*Nora Ephron, director and screenwriter, on her friend, producer Lynda Obst*

When I was two or three years old, I wandered from my house when my mother wasn't looking, intently searching the neighborhood for a friend named Lisa. I don't know anymore who that particular Lisa was, but the memory of looking for a friend named Lisa always stuck in my mind. For me, it was a premonition that someday I'd have a friend named Lisa, and she'd be very important to me.

About fifteen years ago, I met a girl from Canada in a Martha Graham dance class. Lisa Mackie and I shared a love of dance, and we were both studying to be actresses. I liked her sweetness and honesty, and we soon became friends. We had no idea at the time that our friendship would last so long and become so deep.

Through many years, our life directions have been ever-changing, but our friendship remains constant. She is the sister I chose to have in my life. She is my touchstone. She's always there for me when I need her to listen, to be a shoulder to cry on, or to share my glory with. We wish the best for each other and encourage each other's dreams and happiness. This love we share is the most unconditional I've experienced in my life. I always know Lisa loves me, and I love her, without doubt.

—Leslie Reed, legal assistant and singer-songwriter, on her friend
Lisa Mackie, actress and music agency contracts assistant

It was my first year in New York City, and I felt very alone and isolated. I met Leslie in a dance class at the Martha Graham studio, and afterward, as we both lived in the Village, we traveled downtown together. It was friendship in an instant, and has held strong and grown to this day.

Leslie was beautiful, open and expressive, things I've always longed to be, so I was drawn to her right away. Her response to me was very loving—inviting me to family gatherings, including Christmas, and to her family's home on Long Island. Leslie's graciousness and generosity touched a chord in me. Perhaps I needed "a home away from home," and Leslie became like a sister to me.

Leslie was a beacon of warmth. Because I was new in New York, which can be cold and forbidding, and coming from a family that never talked about love, it meant a lot to me to find someone concerned with loving and being loved. Friendship took on a whole new meaning. I was used to having more intellectual discussions, but my talks with Leslie were on a deeper and more emotional level.

Friendship with Leslie has enriched my life immeasurably, and I can only hope that we move into the new millennium together with such grace and compassion.

> —*Lisa Mackie, actress and music agency contracts assistant, on her*
> *friendship with Leslie Reed, legal assistant and singer-songwriter*

My life was dull and monotonous. I had everything, yet my hands were empty. I was walking along the boulevard Raspail with Mama and I suddenly asked myself the agonizing question: "What is happening to me? Is this what my life is to be? Nothing more? And will it always be like this, always?" The idea of living through an infinity of days, weeks, months, and years that were void of hope completely took my breath away: It was as if, without any warning, the whole world had died. But I was unable to give a name to this distress either.

For ten to fifteen days I dragged myself somehow, on legs that seemed as weak as water, from hour to hour, from day to day.

One afternoon I was taking my things off in the cloakroom at school when Zaza came up to me. We began to talk, to relate various things that had happened to us, and to comment on them; my tongue was suddenly loosened, and a thousand bright suns began blazing in my breast; radiant with happiness, I told myself: "That's what was wrong; I needed Zaza!" So total had been my ignorance of the workings of the heart that I hadn't thought of telling myself: "I miss her." I needed her presence to realize how much I needed her.

—*Simone de Beauvoir on her childhood best friend Zaza*

You are one perpetual Achievement; yet you give the impression of having infinite leisure. One comes to see you: you are prepared to spend two hours of Time in talk. One may not, for reasons of health, come to see you: you write divine letters, four pages long. You support mothers, vicariously. You produce books which occupy a permanent place on one's bedside shelf next to Gerald MANLY Hopkins and the Bible. You cast a beam across the dingy landscape of the Times Literary Supplement. You change people's lives. You set up type. You offer to read and criticise one's poems. . . . How is it done?

—Vita Sackville-West in a letter to Virginia Woolf

Friendship is a pledge that covers varying degrees of strength and intensity and is as universal as the smile. We need all kinds of friends—neighbors, high school buddies, work mates, and spouses alike. Whether we swap theories on child rearing over a cup of coffee, or just good mystery novels, all friends offer us the invitation to be ourselves.

. . . Not everyone has the capacity to become your best friend, even though you share with them a special part of you. Best friends reach a higher level, nirvana if you will. It is a meeting of the minds, bound loyalty, and the person you want to go to first with good news or bad. As soul mates, best friends can speak with their eyes— just a knowing glance tells a thousand words. The common ground is endless.

—Dr. Joyce Brothers

We've talked over the years . . . about boyfriends and husbands and children, about hopes and wishes, about careers or the lack of them. We've drunk together—tea, wine, Kool-Aid, even wheat-grass juice when we were going through a phase—and discussed the riddles of the universe. And no matter whether a year or two or six have passed, the threads of our conversation are picked up easily, as though time hasn't hurtled by, as though we're still two kids sitting on the tennis court at the Southside Park, saying, "When I grow up . . ."

—Susan Johnson, writer and bookstore owner, on her longtime friend, Nona

In high school I had a wonderful friend. We shared everything . . . our clothes, our homes, our grades. Our teachers called us the Gold-Dust Twins after a popular laundry soap. When my friend was depressed, I cried. When she was hurt, I bled. When she didn't have a date for Saturday night, I called her from wherever I was having a good time.

We shared something so special that in her yearbook I wrote, "To my most dearest number-1 best friend. Yours till Niagara Falls. All the best in the world, kid. I will never forget you. Your devoted friend."

I can't remember her name.

—Erma Bombeck

My first choice was Kappa Alpha Theta, the same sorority to which Annie Fraser, my friend from New Trier, belonged. I went through the initial day of partying and events. Then, at the end of that evening, I came down with a bad flu, and went straight to bed, thus missing the rest of the week of socializing. As a result, I assumed my chances of pledging a sorority, especially Kappa Alpha Theta, were ruined.

Yet apparently my name was the source of some high drama when the Thetas' selection committee went into its final round of discussion. Somehow I remained in contention, but there were a few girls who wondered if I had the right stuff and asked if I had a recommendation from any Theta alums.

Annie exploded. She ripped off her sorority pin and threw it across the room in disgust. "If you don't pledge Ann-Margret, you don't have me either," she exclaimed. With that, she slammed out of the sorority, a true friend.

A few nights later, Mother came into my room, where I was still in bed with a temperature. The doorbell had rung a few moments earlier, though I hadn't heard it. Mother told me to get out of bed and look outside the window. And there stood the girls from the Theta house on the front lawn, each one holding a lighted candle. Bundled up in a warm robe, I opened the window and tried to say hello, and thanks, but all that came out were tears of joy. My new sorority sisters serenaded me with the Theta song and initiated me on the spot.

> —*Ann-Margret remembering how her friend Annie Fraser fought to get her into her sorority at Northwestern University*

So closely interwoven have been our lives, our purposes and experiences that, separated, we have a feeling of incompleteness—united, such strength of self-assertion that no ordinary obstacles, difficulties or dangers ever appear to us as insurmountable.

> —*Elizabeth Cady Stanton, women's rights activist, in a letter to Susan B. Anthony*

My friend Beth and I used to stand on the street corner and talk for hours on end, all throughout junior high school. She and I did so many crazy things together: screaming contests, riding each other on bicycle handlebars with bare feet in the freezing cold, practicing gymnastic moves everywhere, and sleeping at each other's houses, the perfect occasion for sneaking out at night and running around the village.

We didn't see each other very much during and just after college, but during our twenties got together occasionally. Beth let me borrow the bridesmaids' gowns from her wedding so that my bridesmaids could use them. Now we each have a son and a daughter, almost the same ages. We schedule reunions twice a year at one of our houses, and find that nothing has changed. We love each other and can still talk about everything and nothing for hours on end.

> —*Nancy R. Potter, former packaging engineer (now business assistant and mom), on best friend, Beth Jones La Fave, teacher*

We touch each other through the things we choose to give. We stroke, decorate, adorn and caress one another, both in body and mind. The glorious gift from Honor sits on my mantel—a leather-bound copy of my last book, marbled paper front and back, deep red covers. In this language, we offer each other double kinds of support—the body and the mind, the woman and the work, each part as valuable as the other. A hand touches a hand. A mind reaches out for another mind. Something connects.

—*Louise Bernikow, writer, on her friend, writer Honor Moore*

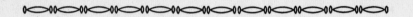

My husband, Arno, met Fritz weeks before I did. We had just adopted our first child at birth and I was determined to nurse him, since I'd read that it was possible to do so. I had been pregnant the year before and had a stillborn baby, followed by three miscarriages. My hormones were still ready to be activated so that I could nurse him.

We enlisted the help of some local moms who'd just had babies. They'd donate mother's milk to me in little baggies each day to supplement mine until I could solely nourish our baby. We had nine milk moms, and Fritz was one of them.

As he picked up the daily baggies, Arno kept telling me how much I would like Fritz. A few weeks later I met her when I brought our son, Joss, to her house. She was everything Arno had told me and more—kind, generous, giving, loving, and devoted. Her oldest son was two months older than Joss and they became best friends.

I could always count on Fritz's great advice and complete devotion. A year and a half later, when I told her we were thinking of adopting another child, she asked, "Are you sure? Because when you decide on something, it always happens so quickly for you." I told her we were sure.

Two days later she phoned to tell me an old friend's daughter was expecting a baby that she planned to have adopted. Fritz told her about me, and that child became our second son, Bowie. Fritz is still my best friend. We talk on the phone often and each Friday go hiking together. We are like sisters and tell each other our deepest secrets, laugh and agonize over life's gifts and challenges. We are so grateful to have each other.

> —*Evelyn Jacob Jaffe, artist and chef, on her dear friend Fritz Pinney*

As teenagers, Carol and I agonized over unrequited crushes and sympathized with each other over our parents' shortcomings. Together, we planned our glorious lives to come as wives, mothers, and celebrities. . . .

[When we met again last August] in her eyes I saw a reflection that made me appear renewedly familiar to myself. The first thing she said to me was, "You're still wearing your hair in bangs, like Audrey Hepburn. You always loved her." And so I had, although I'd completely forgotten about that long-ago crush until Carol reminded me. My old friend remembered facts about me I'd completely shed. It was as if she'd been holding parts of me in trust.

> —*Bette-Jane Raphael, journalist, on her friend Carol*

My heart has just been called back to the time when we used to sit with our arms around each other at the sunset hour & talk & talk of our friends & our homes & of ten thousand subjects of mutual interest until both our hearts felt warmer & lighter for the pure communion of spirit.

> —*Antoinette Brown, women's rights activist, in a letter to Lucy Stone, her "sister under the skin" who became her sister in truth when they married brothers*

A friend is someone you can call in the middle of the night when your man is gone, or you wish he would go, or you suspect your cellulite is winning—or even just to prove to yourself that there is someone you can call in the middle of the night.

—*Anne Beatts, writer*

Melanie does everything with great fanfare. She doesn't just enter a room, she fills it. She comes in like a tall ship with billowing sails entering a harbor; the other boats get out of the way, and their crews stare in reverent admiration. She learned this from her mother, whose tiny frame can barely contain her effervescence.

Melanie's approach to life inspired us deeply, and whenever my parents felt they were getting the runaround from the hospital, they asked, "What would Melanie do?" What Melanie does is whatever she damn well pleases, and if you don't like it, then get out of the way. She doesn't act impetuously or without thinking; but once she decides what needs to be done, she does it. Melanie has always been our fearless leader.

—*Heidi von Beltz, actress and former stuntwoman, on her best friend and staunch supporter through her physical rehabilitation, actress Melanie Griffith*

My God, I love to think of you, Virginia, as my friend. Don't cry me an ardent creature or say, with your head a little on one side, smiling as though you knew some enchanting secret: "Well, Katherine, we shall see..." But pray consider how rare it is to find someone with the same passion for writing that you have.

—*Katherine Mansfield on the gift of Virginia Woolf's friendship*

The progress of the friendship between Catherine and Isabella was quick as its beginning had been warm, and they passed so rapidly through every gradation of increasing tenderness, that there was shortly no fresh proof of it to be given to their friends or themselves. They called each other by their Christian name, were always arm in arm when they walked, pinned up each other's train for the dance, and were not to be divided in the set; and if a rainy morning deprived them of other enjoyments, they were still resolute in meeting in defiance of wet and dirt, and shut themselves up, to read novels together.

—*from* Northanger Abbey *by Jane Austen*

Blatts and I don't think that we look anything alike. Oh, sure, we are both tall, we wear glasses, and we have fair hair, though hers is coppery while mine is golden. But our body shapes are quite different and our eyes and noses and mouths are different, too.

Others, however, have been certain that we are sisters. Years ago, some even insisted that we were twins. Clerks in stores, flight attendants, waitresses, new acquaintances, even strangers on the street would smile knowingly and declare, "You're sisters."

Sometimes we'd truthfully respond, "No." Sometimes we'd only smile slyly. And sometimes we made up stories. We said that Daddy was a bounder and a rogue and that we were born four months apart to different mothers. Or we said that we were born as twins and in a medical miracle Blatts was born four months before me. Even now, after more than thirty years, we are still amazed and amused when we hear the declaration: "You're sisters." We laugh and shake our heads, secure in knowing that we are forever united with deep bonds of love and friendship—sisters by choice.

—Christine Stratton, office manager, on lifelong friend and "twin under the skin" Terri Blattspieler, travel agent

I first met Christine in 1966, while we were both students at Washington State University. We were both going through rush because we'd been "pushed" into it, but we didn't really believe in the fraternal system. Christine was pretty shy, and I was, too, but she sought me out. We ended up pledging the same house and staying for a year, then leaving. But the friendship lasted.

We've been friends for a long time. A few years ago, when my mother was dying, Christine called to ask about her, and if she could come to Montana to be with me. My mother was undergoing treatment for a brain tumor, but she'd made it clear that she did not want to continue in such a miserable way. She told me she wanted to die, and though I could agree with her philosophically, I still had hope. I wasn't ready for her to give up.

As I was talking to Christine, I stood outside my mother's door, listening to the odd sound of her snoring. It was unusual for her to sleep past eight A.M. I told Christine everything that had been happening, but said my mother didn't want to see anyone. As we spoke, I kept pacing throughout the house with the phone. After our conversation, I went into my mother's room. The snoring had stopped and she was dead.

After they took her body away, I called Christine. She was there the next day and knew just what to do. I could not have done it without her. I've never had a friend who would drop everything to help me out.

—Terri Blattspieler, travel agent, on her friend, Christine Stratton

We belonged to a generation of young women who felt extraordinarily free—free from the demand to marry unless we chose to do so, free to postpone marriage while we did other things, free from the need to bargain and hedge that had burdened and restricted women of earlier generations. We laughed at the idea that a woman could be an old maid at twenty-five, and we rejoiced at the new medical care that made it possible for a woman to have a child at forty.

". . . Never break a date with a girl for a man" was one of our mottoes in a period when women's loyalty to women usually was—as it usually still is—subordinate to their possible relationships with men. We learned loyalty to women, pleasure in conversation with women, and enjoyment of the way in which we complemented one another in terms of our differences in temperament, which we found as interesting as the complementarity that is produced by the difference of sex. Throughout extraordinarily different career lines we have continued to enjoy one another, and although meeting becomes more difficult as we scatter in retirement, we continue to meet and take delight in one another's minds.

> —*Margaret Mead, anthropologist, on her circle of women friends in college*

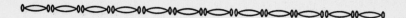

To say old friendships are best is trite, and like so much that is trite, true. Two years ago, I was diagnosed with breast cancer. I learned I would lose both breasts. Carol and Judy flew to New York to be with me, to make me laugh, to let me cry. Other, newer friends were there for me during that time, too. But only Carol and Judy had, as they pointed out, known me before I grew breasts to begin with.

—*Linda Ellerbee*

Friendship between women can take different forms. It can run like a river, quietly and sustainingly through life; it can be an intermittent, sometime thing; or it can explode like a meteor, altering the atmosphere so that nothing ever feels or looks the same again.

—*Molly Haskell, critic and author*

I have heard that memory is 80 percent smell. I don't know if that is a verifiable percentage, but every time I put a piece of rye bread in the toaster, I think of Laurie. I was twelve years old when I discovered that toast didn't have to be white bread. I was sleeping over at my best friend Laurie's house when I first smelled the sharp, singed-caraway aroma of rye toast. I was astonished and laughed at her outrageousness; she was toasting RYE BREAD. Then she made me taste it, and I was hooked. This morning, breakfasting on my rye toast, I realized this was only one small way my best friend had broadened my horizons, and that that's one of the things best friends do best.

> —*Valerie Schultz on her friendship with Laurie that began in third grade*

CELIA: Oh, my poor Rosalind, whither wilt thou go?
Wilt thou change fathers? I will give thee mine.
I charge thee, be not thou more grieved than I am.
ROSALIND: I have more cause.
CELIA: Thou hast not, cousin.
Prithee, be cheerful. Know'st thou not the Duke
Hath banished me, his daughter?
ROSALIND: That he hath not.
CELIA: No, hath not? Rosalind lacks then the love
Which teacheth thee that thou and I am one.
Shall we be sundered? Shall we part, sweet girl?
No, let my father seek another heir.
Therefore devise with me how we may fly,
Whither to go, and what to bear with us.
And do not seek to take your change upon you,
To bear your griefs yourself and leave me out;
For, by this heaven, now at our sorrows pale,
Say what thou canst, I'll go along with thee.

> —*from Shakespeare's* As You Like It.
> *As Rosalind is banished, so will her friend Celia share her exile* . . .

I don't think any woman in power really has a happy life unless she's got a large number of women friends ... because you sometimes must go and sit down and let down your hair with someone you can trust totally.

—*Margaret Thatcher*

I'll never forget how she looked when she opened the door. She was so young I thought she might be someone's daughter. She had three small children and these intense, flashing brown eyes. I don't think she knew a soul in town. I told her who I was and why I was there, and she invited me inside. We sat down and started talking. Almost instantly we realized there was something between us ... a connection. We were both outsiders in a small town, looking for love and acceptance. That was the beginning of an extraordinary friendship.

> —*Laurie Wilkens on first meeting novelist Grace Metalious (who wrote* Peyton Place; *inspired, in part, by stories Wilkens shared about Gilmanton, New Hampshire, where both lived)*

We both feel the same way about teaching: We always tried to make it fun, not annoying, to learn a language; tried to understand our students during the rebellious sixties. (Judy is a French professor; I taught German for many years.) We are almost a generation apart in age. I am the older one, but that never seemed to matter.

The time we spend together is always special. When I was living in Brussels because of my husband's work, she and her husband came to visit us. And I would stay with her part of each summer in Ohio. Both of us like to cook and bake. The best apple pie I ever ate we baked together.

She has a lovely home near the university where she teaches now, and that was where I went after the demise of my marriage. I was heartbroken, and nobody except my youngest son helped me as much as Judy did during that painful time. She read poetry to me, walked and swam with me, and was never impatient with my grieving. I can never thank her enough for that rare understanding.

Why is Judy such a special friend? I admire her keen intellect combined with the greatest sensitivity of heart and her down-to-earth approach to life. I wish everyone could have a friend like Judy.

—Irene Williams, retired teacher, on her longtime friendship with Judy Cochran, Ph.D.

When the willow bends at the first hint of troubled breezes, our friends come running to see how they can help.

Sometimes friends know when they are needed even before we realize it ourselves, because we are accustomed to letting them in on the happenings of our lives. Similarly, they trust and confide in us. We dissect, inspect, and respect all our relationships—and give both welcome and unwelcome advice to one another. We know about each other's troubled kids, troubling parents, and shaky marriages because our friends share their concerns and their triumphs. We don't keep too many secrets from true friends.

—*Lois Wyse, author and advertising executive*

It's been sixty-plus years, but the picture in my mind is as clear as if it were yesterday. Looking out the living-room window of our third floor apartment on 78th Street, between Constance and Bennett in Chicago, I see my best friend, Mary, fat curls bobbing beneath her straw hat, walking to Sunday School on Easter Sunday.

We used to have peanut butter and lemonade picnics under a tablecloth spread over a card table in her backyard. Our apartment building had only a paved back courtyard where people hung their wash. Her mother made donuts, and we got to eat the holes.

Mary and I spent summer days at the beach, ice-skated in the winter, played run-sheep-run with the rest of the gang on warm summer nights. We stalked boyfriends, mourned lost loves, wrote to the same soldier during the war. She married him.

The dress she made for my small daughter, a creation of blue velvet and white organdy, is stored carefully, wrapped in tissue paper. A keepsake.

Years passed, letters were few. One day her husband's business brought them to California, and then Mary and her two daughters to my town. It was Sunday School, backyard picnics, confidences, all over again, as though we had never parted.

> —*Carol Ann Johnson, retired nurse-educator, recalling her childhood
> friend Mary Louise Collosky-Whitford*

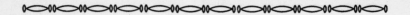

Once you're out of school, you'll see that it's easy to forget about the need for friends because there is an interesting man or an interesting job or the complexities of raising children, but maintaining friendships is an important thing. A friendship is not like the bond with a husband or brother; it's different. Even if you don't see each other, the tie is there.

>   —*Nina Totenberg, National Public Radio commentator, in a speech*
>   *to students at Chatham College*

Mary Jo and I had both lived in New York for more than just a couple of years. However, one day we came to the realization that we had no friends. Well, we had *some* friends, but not *a lot* of friends, which we were accustomed to having when we were growing up in Kansas and Illinois. Not enough friends that we could call on the spur of the moment to come over and chat, or go get half-price concert tickets or take a walk down Broadway. Always women-of-action, we took matters into our own hands and established Friendly Fridays. The idea was to invite a few friends over on a Friday night for pizza and beer. The only price of admission was to bring a friend. (No wonder we had no friends; our culinary tastes were no enticement!) We did this for a few Fridays over the course of a couple of months. The result? We were never quite sure if we made any more friends, but our Friday nights were a helluva lot more fun!

>   —*Colleen Wyse*, Glamour *magazine beauty director, on her friend*
>   *and cohost, Mary Jo Dondlinger, theatrical lighting designer*

There is a moment when we are searching for a place of belonging when we see ourselves in the glass of our lives—a liquid presence staring back at us, a reminder of our presence in the world. What confirms our existence is not just the reflection. If we merely had to see ourselves, to be affirmed, we would be narcissists, needing only a house of mirrors to comfort us. It is seeing our image merge with that of someone approaching from the outside that affirms who we are.

—*Connie Porter, novelist*

She made me believe in myself. She was hysterically loud and loved noise and a good time. She made me feel okay to be who I was. My family never made me feel this way. . . .

I had no money. I had absolutely nothing. I got a quarter a week for allowance. What are you going to do with a quarter a week? So my girlfriend said, "This is what I do." So I said I'd do it with her. But I didn't really like it. It was too terrifying. It hurt my nerves. . . . After my girlfriend and I took this makeup—lipsticks and hair dye—from the mall, we were on our way home with our little bags. It was pouring rain—we were in the middle of a hurricane—and my girlfriend and I got down on our knees and said, "God, if you don't kill us in this hurricane we swear we will never do this again." We didn't die and we never did it again. I keep my vows.

—*Bette Midler, on her friend (and, briefly, partner-in-crime) Beth Ellen Childers*

1993, a watershed year for me in terms of self-discovery. Most amazing was the revelation of my own true nature—I was a bad girl at heart. All it took to convert me was a writer's conference, an award for sensuality, and two deliciously daring new friends. What Renaissance women they were. Before I knew it, I was in a ménage à trois of friendship and loving every minute of it. The Bad Girls' Club was born.

Anna Eberhardt, Olivia Rupprecht, and I had never set eyes on each other before that night, but we had several things in common. We were all up for the "Most Sensual Writer" award; we shared the same taste in shoes—mile-high chickadee wedgies; and we had the same distaste for competition. The way we clicked was astonishing. We were meant to meet and change each other's lives. There was only one way to deal with the contest, we decided. We couldn't rig the outcome. So—I got to win the award, but it cost me a Queen's ransom in Godiva. Small payment for the value, I realized, and with every year that passes, I gain a deeper, richer understanding of what our connection meant. Friendship was the trophy we all took away that night.

> —*Suzanne Forster, fiction writer, on a group friendship that*
> *"sizzles"*

She is a person of deep family feeling, "grappling" her children and grandchildren to her heart with "hoops of steel," and she can be counted on by her friends for loyalty and devotion, warmth and practical assistance in good and bad times. I asked her if she would read a poem at Steve's funeral. I know this kind of "appearance" is nerve-racking for her, but she loved Steve and came through with a perfectly beautiful reading of Conrad Aiken's "Music I Hear with You." And recently, when I was hit with another dreadful blow, my son's death, she arrived full of love—and with enough Chinese food for an army for a week—to comfort me, my daughter, and other close friends who were gathered around me.

I have snapshots of her singing at our twenty-fifth wedding anniversary party and at her East Hampton home, and she looks great in all of them. As far as I can see, there isn't a bad angle or even a second best angle, even as the years advance and she has four grandchildren's birthday parties to go to.

Whatever she is doing, shooting a Robert Altman film in Paris, hosting an important benefit, or insisting in her unmistakable deep contralto on TV that you have "some Royal Caribbean coming," or just calling me up on the phone to say "hello," I know I have a very glamorous friend.

> —*Betty Comden, Broadway lyricist and librettist, on her friend Lauren Bacall*

The strange thing, on looking back, was the purity, the integrity, of her feeling for Sally. It was not like one's feeling for a man. It was completely disinterested, and besides, it had a quality which could only exist between women, between women just grown up. It was protective, on her side, sprang from a sense of being in league together, a presentiment of something which was bound to part them (they spoke of marriage always as a catastrophe), which led to this chivalry, this protective feeling which was much more on her side than Sally's. For in those days she was completely reckless; did the most idiotic things out of bravado; bicycled round the parapet on the terrace; smoked cigars. Absurd, she was—very absurd. But the charm was overpowering, to her at least, so that she could remember standing in her bedroom at the top of the house holding the hot-water can in her hands and saying aloud, "She is beneath this roof . . . She is beneath this roof!"

—*from* Mrs. Dalloway *by Virginia Woolf*

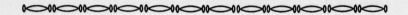

Of my dear Sarah—I believe one of her noblest qualities was her great generosity. Others could only guess at this, but I was allowed to know it. Not that she made gifts, but a wide sympathy was hers for every disappointed or incompetent fellow creature. It was a most distinguishing characteristic! Governor Andrew spoke of Judge B——once as "A friend to every man who did not need a friend!" Sarah's quick sympathy knew a friend was in need before she knew it herself; she was the spirit of beneficence, and her quick delicate wit was such a joy in daily companionship!

> —*Annie Fields, writer and wife of the editor of* The Atlantic, *on her dearest friend, writer Sarah Orne Jewett*

I wonder if you really send
  Those dreams of you that come and go!
I like to say, "She thought of me,
  And I have known it." Is it so?

Though other friends walk by your side,
  Yet sometimes it must surely be,
They wonder where your thoughts have gone,
  Because I have you here with me.

And when the busy day is done
  And work is ended, voices cease,
When every one has said good night,
  In fading firelight, then in peace

I idly rest: you come to me—
  Your dear love holds me close to you.
If I could see you face to face
  It would not be more sweet and true

*—Sarah Orne Jewett, who wrote "Together" to honor her beloved
friend Annie Fields (1875)*

Some people simply seem to know how to live. They know when to seize the day, when to go with the flow, and when to row for dear life. My friend Jan Munson was such a person. She had incredible instincts and knew how to listen to them. One year well after we turned thirty, she decided her life needed changing. After years of working late nights in bars and restaurants, she longed to be a morning person. Landlocked in reality, she knew she'd sleep better near the ocean. Jan loathed exercise, calling us both serious slugs amid workout bumblebees. But, determined to become a scuba instructor, she pursued fitness as surely as she had commanded sloth. Certification in hand, my friend moved to the Florida Keys, pursued her dream, and called each year during lobster season to cheerfully taunt me.

Jan's gifts to me have translated quite literally into these words. I had been to college and worked a variety of interesting jobs before shifting gears to have children. I always thought I'd take better care of myself a bit later in my life, find time for my music, and fulfill my lifelong goal of being a professional writer. Someday. Then Jan went to the beach and I was jolted out of my *mañana* mentality. I sold my first piece of writing shortly thereafter. My scratchy vinyl albums have given way to a growing collection of compact discs. Nowadays I even walk for fitness and find it a pleasure.

Jan's untimely death to cancer just reaffirmed the lessons her life taught me: Talent's important and education, too, but in the real world, life's short, so keep the focus sharp and do what you know in your heart is right.

> —*Nel Newman, writer and radio host, remembering her friend Jan Munson*

Although, ultimately, each of us is alone in life, my friend helps me feel less alone. While my husband is a companion by my side on the journey, my friend is the one who helps me sort through it all. Sharing my experiences with her both comforts me and helps me to grow. We have fun together; we help each other; but, above all, it is our talking that makes my life fuller.

With my friend I can reveal more of myself than I do with most other people: my uncertainties, my observations, my regrets, my wit, my despair, my achievements. Beyond sharing the highs and lows of life, we share the details, the ordinary stuff that we know is interesting only to those who truly know and care about us: what we're making for dinner, what we'd like to do with our homes, what the doctor recommended for one of our sick kids, how we're planning on cutting our hair.

To share both the sublime and the minutiae takes trust that we won't be judged; with most people it seems we stick more in the middle ground, talking about things that have more universal interest, and feel somehow safer. But with my friend Lisa, I am more fully myself.

> —*Katharine Canfield, editor and mother of two, on her friend and*
> *fellow parent Lisa Levine*

We're inexhaustible shoppers. We go to a million flea markets—we're flea marketeers! One of my last great finds was a wooden footstool carved in the shape of a horseshoe that says "Good Luck" on it. Actually I wasn't so sure about it until Karlene talked me into it—that's what best friends are for!

We're best friends for the long haul. In fact, one of the jokes we have is what color our hair will be when we're seventy. Karlene's blond, so we figure she'll be platinum by then. I want to have jet-black like Morticia Addams.

—*Julia Louis-Dreyfus on her best friend Karlene*

"You know, I been thinking about going." Pat looked at me from between the fringes of her bangs. "Thinking about dumping school completely and running off. Find me some real dope and people who an't planning on working at the Winn Dixie the rest of their lives."

It was a conversation we'd had dozens of times. We'd talked about running off until we knew just how to go about it. We'd memorize the bus fares for all the cities we were considering, and played at making up false IDs. Sometimes it was only the game that kept us from actually buying the Trailways ticket out of town. This time should have been no different from any other. I should have chimed in with my own curses, said, "Damn, yes, let's go."

But I did not. There was something in Pat's voice, some edge of frustration. Her eyes were turned away, but I could see just how dark and bright they had become. She's going to do it, I thought, and shocked myself with a wave of desperate longing. The rush of my need stunned me—not to go with her but to keep her with me. Suddenly I understood that more than anything in the world I did not want Pat to disappear out of my life into some strange Yankee city, some alien life where I could not follow. My mouth opened, and I barely stopped myself from begging her to stay.

—*Dorothy Allison, novelist and memoirist*

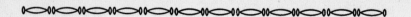

... My girlfriends filled my days with the steady pulse of constant companionship. What did we do? Mostly, I think, we talked. We talked on the buses, in the halls, at our lockers, in the classrooms, after school at the bus stop. Once home, we called up one another almost instantly and talked on the phone until some parent couldn't stand it any longer. What on earth, our parents asked us, did we find to talk about? But it wasn't so much the topics we found engrossing, I think—the boys, teachers, clothes, gossip. All that talking built up a steady confidence that the trivia of our lives were worth discussion, that our lives were worth discussing. "Do you think I ought to get my hair cut?" was a question that asked not only, "How would I look with my hair shorter?" but "Do you *care* how I look?" Teachers snapped and lectured; parents discussed and argued; boys teased and muttered; but the steady hum of girl friends, punctuated by laughter and whispers, was a reassuring continuo.

—Susan Allen Toth recalling her dear friends of girlhood

Because we'd been friends since the fifth grade, I was naturally upset to miss her wedding. But my first child, a daughter, had arrived earlier that morning, January 27, 1962. My daughter's middle name would be my friend's first name: Joyce.

Imagine my surprise to see my redheaded wacky friend and her new husband, both still in their wedding clothes, walking through the door of my room in the maternity ward. "Just checking it out," she quipped to the amused staff. "Wanted to see my namesake." She brought cake, too.

Years later, on their apartment balcony overlooking the island of Zamalek in Cairo, we both listened as the mullahs recited the evening prayers over the loudspeakers. We both giggled out loud. "Look where we are—two punks from Levittown." Travel has been a great part of our lives. We've each had a career and traveled independently, she to Russia, China, Ukraine, Africa; I to India, Thailand, and the Philippines.

Yet we still share our ideas and information as we did as kids. Time has not altered our relationship. We don't always agree. Never did. We depend on each other for balance, and in an odd way challenge intellectually our ideas and actions. And, of course, each of us thinks she is right.

In 1994, on that same January 27, arriving home after a stay in Florida, I heard my answering machine deliver a sad message from Joyce: Her mom, who had raised four children alone, had unexpectedly died that morning.

Now this date has become a bittersweet occasion for us, but surely bonds us even closer as the years go by.

—*Marianne Vecsey, painter, on her friend Joyce Lannert*

There was a great deal of natural antagonism at first between Nan Watts and me. Unfortunately, but in the fashion of the day, we had each been given harangues about the other by our respective families. Nan, who was a gay, boisterous tomboy, had been told how nicely Agatha always behaved, "so quiet and polite." And while Nan had my decorum and general solemnity praised to her, *I* had been admonished on the subject of Nan, who was said to be "never shy, always answered when she was spoken to—never flushed, or muttered, or sat silent." We both therefore looked at each other with a great deal of ill will.

A sticky half-hour ensued, and then things livened up. In the end we organized a kind of steeplechase round the schoolroom, doing wild leaps from piled-up chairs and landing always on the large and somewhat elderly chesterfield. We were all laughing, shouting, screaming, and having a glorious time. Nan revised her opinion of me—here was somebody anything but quiet, shouting at the top of her voice. I revised my opinion of Nan as being stuck-up, talking too much, and "in" with the grown-ups. We had a splendid time, we all liked each other, and the springs of the sofa were permanently broken. . . .

Nan went to live in Ireland, I lived in London. Later Nan lived in London, too, and we came together again. Then in the Second World War, Nan sent her daughter to me in Devon for shelter, and arrived herself finally to take a house nearby in Devon. Nan is one of the friends I miss most now.

—*Agatha Christie recalling how she met her lifelong friend Nan Watts*

In a world of relationships that come with conditions and strings attached, where a straight answer is hard to come by and the truth an even scarcer commodity, a close friend is one of life's most profound Reality Checks. She calls the shots as she sees them, usually sees them clearly, knows exactly who you are, never forgets, sometimes reminds you, too. She knows how wonderful you are, and will tell you so over and over when you need to hear it. She knows the games you play and won't hesitate to tell you when she thinks you're screwing up.

—*Carol Lynn Mithers, journalist*

I walked to school every day with a girl who lived across the street from us, a girl by the name of Jean, and I adored her. We were as different from each other as her family and household were different from mine. Our walks to school every morning would have been sheer delight to me if school had not been at the other end; and there was one other little unpleasantness, I was always afraid of being late. . . . I was up and dressed and over calling for Jean long before she sat down at table for her breakfast. I went crazy with nervousness watching her and waiting; at the same time I was fascinated by her slow and elegant movements and by the fact that she did not worry at all about being late. That seemed singularly aristocratic. . . .

The grandmother poured coffee from a splendid silver pot, and served the bacon from a silver platter. The slices slithered around on the shiny surface and her old hands trembled, but she caught them eventually. It all took time, and I don't know why I tortured myself waiting, except that Jean was the bright necessity of my life. . . .

—Aline Bernstein, costume designer, recalling her closest childhood
friend, Jean

I like to play with my friend Alexandra, who's in my class at school. We make up mystery stories and act them out. We even started a friendship club just for the two of us. We talk about stuff, play games, read books together, and draw. I like mysteries and she likes imaginary stories. I can make her laugh by being silly and telling her jokes.

My cousin Darlene is also one of my best friends, even though she lives near San Francisco. When we're together, we like jumping on her trampoline. Last time we went walking to the place she calls her "secret garden." To get there, we crossed a little river and picked up rocks. We got a little dirty but we had fun.

I have four or five close friends at school, but sometimes we argue or get mad. The other day we all wanted to go on the same swing, and so we had a big, big fight. I decided to work it out by not going on the swing and doing something else.

A real friend doesn't give you put-downs or hurt your feelings. A friend gives put-ups, gives you compliments, and makes you feel good.

> —*Taylor Aston-Nielsen, age seven going on eight, California second-grader*

She first came into my life at school, but as she was one class ahead of me, I never knew her well. Then she married my cousin Edwin Loeb. That didn't work, and Benita and I made her get a divorce. When she came to London she was just recovering from her divorce. She had not as yet got into any further trouble. Laurence loved her, and I was delighted as she was my oldest friend. She is hard to describe, because she was so elusive. If you ever pinned her down to anything you would find out the next day she had told someone else the exact opposite of what she had told you. She saw around and into everything. . . . She looked like a Cheshire cat because she had an enormous mouth which was perpetually grinning. She was extremely stubborn. She seemed to know what she wanted in life, but she didn't at all really know what was good for her. For some strange reason she always had the wrong husband, and she had three of them. As a mother she was a great success, and had lots of pleasure from her three children. . . . Peggy never failed to appear at the crucial moments in my life. I felt all I had to do was to bring out my Aladdin's lamp and Peggy would pop up and help me.

—*Peggy Guggenheim, arts patron, on her best friend, Peggy*

Gayle was so miserable that her good Baptist parents considered enrolling her in Catholic school. But on a day the class had to choose partners for an outing to the park, Gayle decided not to be left alone again. She chose Patty, the other girl nobody ever picked, and a friendship began. To Gayle, Pat seemed like she knew things, and she never seemed lonely or worried, even when she was by herself. And Gayle let Pat into her fantasy world, where anything was possible and it was okay to be a child. . . .

Now in fifth grade, the unlikely twosome was inseparable. The very children who had disliked Gayle because she was so pretty were eventually drawn to her for the same reason. Pat had all but lost her Carolina drawl, but brains didn't make you popular. She was quiet and a little too bookish, but she could be funny sometimes, she always had the right answers to math homework, and her inexplicable closeness to Gayle sealed her acceptance.

> —*from* Tryin' to Sleep in the Bed You Made *by Virginia DeBerry and Donna Grant*

It is said, if you have one good friend, you are lucky...a friend who will listen with understanding (not be too critical), offer her help (no request needed), for whom no call is at the wrong time, and most of all, who comes through with a smile or hug to assure you a brighter day is coming. When the brighter day comes... having a friend to share in the joy and pleasure makes it better!

Well, I'm more than lucky, I'm blessed—with three such good friends.

Millie was a fledgling skier, scared, stranded on a hill. All courage had left her when I came by and asked, "Can I help?" That was the beginning of a friendship that has lasted more than twenty years.

Anneliese is also a skier, and we have shared many a fall. She also lived on the same block as I do. Friendships are sometimes strengthened over something minute; for us, that something was a heating pad. I had taken some bad falls skiing that day, so when Anneliese called late that evening, I shared my woes about bruises and aches. I did not have a heating pad. Well, although it was late and cold, ten minutes later a heating pad arrived! A small thing, but large. No asking, just doing.

Ann is the traveler, who later became a close confidant. We worked for the same organization. When, more than twenty years ago, I commented that I wanted to go to Italy, Ann simply piped up, "When?" We were compatible, enjoyed so many of the same things—browsing through stores, walking, all the cultural stuff, and yes, even the traveling.

My best girlfriends—I hope they feel the same about me.

> *—Marion Scott, retired secretary and New York City Marathon*
> *volunteer, on her three dearest friends*

I was right on time, even a bit early, but she was always there before me (no matter how early one arrived, Marianne was always there first) and, I saw at once, not very tall and not in the least intimidating. She was forty-seven, an age that seemed old to me then, and her hair was mixed with white to a faint rust pink, and her rust-pink eyebrows were frosted with white. The large flat black hat was as I'd expected it to be. She wore a blue tweed suit that day, as she usually did then, a man's "polo shirt," as they were called, with a black bow at the neck. The effect was quaint, vaguely Bryn Mawr 1909, but stylish at the same time. I sat down and she began to talk.

It seems to me that Marianne talked to me steadily for the next thirty-five years, but of course that is nonsensical. I was living far from New York many of those years and saw her at long intervals. She must have been one of the world's greatest talkers: entertaining, enlightening, fascinating, and memorable; her talk, like her poetry, was quite different from anyone else's in the world. I don't know what she talked about at the first meeting; I wish I had kept a diary. Happily ignorant of the poor Vassar girls before who hadn't passed muster, I began to feel less nervous and even spoke some myself. I had what may have been an inspiration, I don't know— at any rate, I attribute my great good fortune in having known Marianne as a friend in part to it. Ringling Bros. and Barnum & Bailey Circus was making its spring visit to New York and I asked Miss Moore (we called each other "Miss" for over two years) if she would care to go to the circus with me the Saturday after next. I didn't know that she *always* went to the circus, wouldn't have missed it for anything.

> —*Elizabeth Bishop, writer, on the early days of her long friendship with poet Marianne Moore*

We laughed, we laughed everywhere together. We mapped out a small colorful universe with our laughter.

We were best friends. It had been a while since I'd had one. I was just eighteen—we both were—and I'd forgotten the strength and joy of that companionship. I had other friends, friends who seemed more adult and sophisticated, political friends: cool friends. This friendship cut through all those pretensions, reached straight back to childhood. We brought each other candy (I remember a bag of Raisinets pinned to my door). We rubbed each other's heads when they were sore and tired. We left cryptic notes for each other in coded languages, in the Mandarin she was learning, in our private girlspeak. We didn't talk about sex.

> —*Sylvia Brownrigg, journalist and fiction writer, on her college best friend*

I believe with all my heart that God put her in my life for a special reason. She came during one of the darkest times. I'm not a demonstrative person, but Tina taught me how to hug. She taught me how to experience life without being afraid of being hurt. Tina has proven her love for me again and again. She knows my dreams, my fears, my hopes—no one knows my soul like Tina.

—*Sharon Holland, television reporter, on her friend, teacher Tina Laido*

When Pam gives me presents, she often gives me food, a pretty bag filled with jars and tins of exotic edibles. And I often give her food, like a huge jar of organic strawberry granola, then wonder later if she ate it or foisted it off on her kids. Pam is seriously thin, fast, vibrant, like something's burning inside, and she takes evasive action by steering into the center of the physical or emotional energy. Many times, she's said astounding things to me in less than the fifty-minute hour, and I'm not even expected to pay her. Talk between women friends is always therapy, but Pam has access to depths of feeling and insight I seem to approach the long way around. . . .

—*Jayne Anne Phillips, novelist and essayist*

LOVE AND FRIENDSHIP

Love is like the wild rose-briar,
Friendship is like the holly-tree—
The holly is dark when the rose-briar blooms
But which will bloom most constantly?

The wild rose-briar is sweet in spring,
In summer blossoms scent the air,
Yet wait till winter comes again
And who will call the wild-briar fair?

Then scorn the silly rose-wreath now
And deck thee with the holly's sheen,
That when December blights thy brow
He still may leave thy garland green.

—Emily Brontë (1839)

My friend has taught me a new way to love. She opened me up to a world of transformation and magic. Before I knew her, I lived largely in a world of "No, you can't!" My lesson from her was "Yes, you can!" And when situations in my life were rocky, I would try to isolate myself. She came to me then and through her life shared what true friendship was really all about. But for me the most important gift thus far I've received from her has been learning to love *me*, and to be a friend to myself. Now I know what it means to have been blessed by an angel. She's my friend.

> —*Akosua Williams, New York artist, on her friendship with Esperanza Martell, clinical social worker*

I have always measured my life by the lives of my best women friends. In seventh grade, when it became time for Susan to begin thinking about men, it was time also for me to begin considering a personal life. My sense of order has come from sharing a well-considered point of view. If in high school Kathy decided so-and-so was crazy for befriending so-and-so, it was in fact a truth. There is nothing as comforting as knowing two opinions are right, to hell with what everyone else thinks.

> —*Wendy Wasserstein*

I met my best friend Lyn at sixteen, thanks to the Easy Method Driving School. When my teacher, Mr. Wilcox, a ringer for Mr. Peepers, showed me her photo and asked if I knew her, I recognized Lyn from high school and wondered what the old guy was doing with her picture. Not that the shot was anything *Playboy* would have printed. It turned out Lyn had taken driving classes from Mr. Wilcox, too. Thanks to him, she and I became lifelong friends.

That year, Lyn and I were in two classes together, Drama and Phys. Ed, though we'd only spoken once or twice before Mr. Wilcox's remark. One of those times, Lyn had crossed the locker room after P.E. to tell me I had the best legs in the class, and I said, "Hey, you're not my type."

We still laugh about that. We still laugh about our summer in Bucks County studying method acting, our summer waitressing in the Catskills, and our trip to Europe after college during which Lyn cornered a handsome blond Dane at the Pussycat Club and talked his head off. I always say that with his limited English, he had no idea they'd just gotten engaged. They've been married now for twenty-three years.

Our mothers were friends. I'm close to her kids. Lyn's in my will to raise my dogs and cats if I die.

We still dream about the day we can once again travel together— when her kids are independent, when we both have more time. We accept that life has changed our bodies, given us double chins, made us too old for discos, made us yearn for the past. But if I had cancer or my husband left me, I know she'd be the first person I'd call.

—*Jill Shure, writer, on her friend Lyn Larsen, English teacher*

What do you say about a friendship that has spanned three decades? What magical ingredients mix together to form and preserve the bonds of that friendship? Certainly love, loyalty, respect, and generosity of spirit all go into the mix; but when I think of my best friend Jill, laughter comes to mind. So often our laughter has been the chicken soup that has nourished, cheered, and healed us. A friendship such as ours is truly food for the soul.

> —*Lyn Larsen, English teacher, on her friendship with writer Jill Shure*

I think what astounds us people of the screen and theatre about her is the number and intensity of her interests. Would it be disloyal to my profession to hint that great stars are apt to show a little more interest in themselves than in anything else? Not Miss Barrymore. It's the world she's interested in—or rather a lot of different worlds—sports, history, music, politics, books. It seems impossible that a human being with the austere allowance of only twenty-four hours every day can keep in such close touch with them.

She has more friends than anyone I know, but she's not a dear, gentle soul. Barrymores don't come like that. She has a trenchant wit, she can rebuke stupidity, or intolerance with silence better than Joe Louis could do it with his fists. She makes appallingly accurate observations. She doesn't know the meaning of fear or the meaning of caution. . . .

—*Katharine Hepburn, on her longtime friend Ethel Barrymore*

Some time ago I was on a long day's hike in the mountains with an old friend. We have known each other more than 25 years, and our intimacy is based as much on the numberless small events in our lives as it is on some of the major life dramas we've shared. The weather turned gray and threatening in late morning, and it became obvious that if we didn't stop for lunch soon, we would be eating wet sandwiches. We chose a log under a large tree and sat down.

As I watched my friend huddle over her sandwich in the vain attempt to shield herself from the wind, I felt a sudden surge of pleasure and gratitude. "Aren't old friends wonderful?" I said. She looked up without surprise, answered "Yes," and returned to her sandwich. There was no need for either of us to say anything else.

—Bonnie Kreps, journalist, on a cherished longtime friend

I turn to you, who have known pain and fear
And failure and despair, and in your eyes
I read companionship; and though your cloak
Be threadbare, half of it is mine.
You are my friend.

—Lilla Cabot Perry, painter and poet

My female friends (one of whom I always threaten to marry should I ever decide to kick my husband out) are my greatest source of pleasure, inspiration, and compassion.

When I met JoAnn, we belonged to a school of meditation and self-realization. We both had been involved for about twenty years, but didn't know each other. Then the school had a reunion in Hawaii. I sat down at the pool next to this woman and started talking, and that was it: I just felt that I had found a sister. Somebody I knew totally. It's been about seven years since that moment, and we've not let go of each other. We do anything we can, find any excuse, for me to visit her in Canada or for her to come down here. And the husbands are friends too.

We both have children in their twenties, and even though they're out of the house, there's still *sturm und drang*. With her I can release all those feelings of guilt and fury and resentment and love and pride. I know exactly what she's talking about when she tells me about her daughter, even if my child may not have done exactly the same thing. But because it's not my child, I can be more objective and help her get through it.

My daughter has always wanted to quantify my love for her. "How much do you love me? Would you do this? Would you do that?" So finally one day I said to her, "Carolyn, I would give you one of my kidneys, if you needed it." That's now the bottom line. I'd give JoAnn a kidney.

> —Amy Musher, *Chief,* Time *magazine letters division, on her friend (and partner in an antiques business called "What's Need Got to Do with It") JoAnn Griffin, psychotherapist*

During the first three months, I thought she should establish 1-800-CALL KATE for new mothers. You'd say anything to her, like, "I don't think these are the right size diapers," and suddenly you'd hear *beep-beep-beep*, and a truck would be pulling up. And a deliveryman would say, "Here's 95,000 diapers from Ms. Capshaw."

My son came home from the hospital apparently circumcised. I'm changing him and going, "It doesn't look circumcised." I thought maybe there was some genital configuration that changes at puberty; I didn't know. So Kate came over and said, "Why didn't you have him circumcised?" and I said, "I did." And she was like, "You didn't." And now I'm, like, crying, "I did . . . I really did . . ." So she called the head of OB-GYN at Cedars-Sinai, who is also a moyl, and he came over and performed a bris the very next day.

—*Rosie O'Donnell on her friend, actress Kate Capshaw*

When I first met Dr. G, my friend Gloria, my self-esteem was lower than low. I'd been forced to retire from a job I loved, I hadn't gotten over the death of my first husband, and felt totally dependent on other people to make decisions for me. Our friendship began as a doctor-patient relationship, but over the past ten years it has deepened into something greater than that.

She's been my closest confidant, the person who gave me back my confidence in myself, who sustained me through the painful death of my sister, who taught me to take on the world and become the person I wanted to be. She's given me courage as only a best friend can.

And, where we once shared many struggles through terrible times, now we share the pleasure of collecting McCoy pottery.

> —*Nancy Spruill, antiques dealer and pottery collector, on her friend, Gloria Gurdziel, M.D.*

. . . You know the optimistic directive you've been hearing since the day your folks packed you off to summer camp applies: Don't worry, you'll make new friends. And you will. But no matter how much you change or how many new friends enter your life, old friendships are not replaceable. They are as complex and memorable as any great romantic liaison and should hold as significant a place in your heart. The same old requirements are called for: communication, trust, and attention.

> —*Mary McNamara, Los Angeles writer, on sustaining long-distance friendships after she moved west*

I met my best friend Lee Ann at a church meeting for self-proclaimed skeptics and non-believers. It was and is one of the most powerful ties that bind us: our mutual search for spiritual things that goes beyond conventional wisdom. We also enjoy a good, silly laugh together over many of the absurd things we have done and seen others do, including the actions of our respective husbands. (We try to laugh about them in private.)

Over the past decade we have spent New Year's Eves together, gotten married the same summer, moved apart, had children, gained and lost jobs and family members, alternately celebrated and tried to make sense of our marriages, sipped gin and tonics every summer on the beach, and run up enormous phone bills from time to time. I consider with amazement that our friendship has not only survived all this but apparently flourished, too. Without trying, we seem to have much of what the best marriages have, without too many emotional strings—an understanding of each other's life journey even when it is different from our own, complementary gifts (I am perhaps more volatile and creative; she, brightly analytical and provocative), and a desire to remain committed to our relationship for a long, long time.

It's nice, of course, that our husbands get along well, and that our two families have children about the same age. But it's when we're alone that I get the most from Lee Ann—her unexpected laughter, honest opinions, compassion, and intelligence. Although we may never live in the same town again, we'll always know we're family, two renegade spirits who want to make some sense of life, but who mostly like just living it together.

—*Katharine Roberts, editor and writer, on her best friend Lee Ann Patterson, international agricultural economist*

I averaged three trips a week to the movies. Sometimes I saw as many as eight second runs in five days if Nanny and I hit the boulevard on keno night at the Admiral. We'd get in before one or six, so we could "beat the prices." Ilomay and I would get together on Saturdays and then come home and play the movies we'd just seen. Lots of jungle stuff—Nyoka, queen of the jungle, and Sheena (another queen of the jungle)—lots of pirate stuff—Tyrone Power— and *lots* of Betty Grable. I had the upper hand in our relationship because Ilomay always played the second leads.

Nanny liked Ilomay. She made us capes out of pillowcases, and we dyed them black and tied the strings she sewed on the edges around our necks. We'd put on our black Long Ranger masks we'd bought at the dime store and run like the wind down Cahuenga Boulevard, with our capes flapping behind us. We'd come to a screeching halt when we got to the Bank of America, where we'd flatten ourselves up against the building and hang around most of the afternoon, on the lookout for robbers.

—*Carol Burnett on her childhood best friend Ilomay Sills*

We lived on Yucca Street. Carol lived in one building, and I lived in the other. I lived on the third floor, and she lived on the first floor, so when I left home to go to school, I'd go out of the apartment and go downstairs, pick Carol up, so if we ever had a fight, it always seemed like it was up to me to make up because I'd be the one'd come by her apartment to go to school. I was glad to do it. . . .

We used to play Tarzan. All those Tarzan yells that Carol does on TV were for real. Sheena . . . Nyoka. She was always the boss, but I didn't mind. We had a lot of fun. We used to swing from our legs and give our little Tarzan yells. . . . We were supposed to be watching her little sister, Christine; we'd make sure that she was okay; then we'd go around to the different apartment doors and listen in. We were detectives.

> —*Ilomay Sills on the neighbor and best friend who grew up to be actress and comedienne Carol Burnett*

... The girl had moved her as she had never been moved, and the power to do that, from whatever source it came, was a source that one must admire. Her emotion was still acute, however much she might speak to her visitor as if everything that had happened seemed to her natural; and what kept it, above all, from subsiding was her sense that she found here what she had been looking for so long—a friend of her own sex with whom she might have a union of soul. It took a double consent to make a friendship, but it was not possible that this intensely sympathetic girl would refuse ...

"Will you be my friend, my friend of friends, beyond every one, everything, forever and forever?" Her face was full of eagerness and tenderness.

Verena gave a laugh of clear amusement, without a shade of embarrassment or confusion. "Perhaps you like me too much."

"Of course I like you too much! When I like, I like too much. But of course it's another thing, your liking me," Olive Chancellor added. "We must wait—we must wait. When I care for anything, I can be patient." She put out her hand to Verena, and the movement was at once so appealing and so confident that the girl instinctively placed her own in it.

—*from* The Bostonians *by Henry James*

Vivian has always been the greatest supporting player anyone could ask for. During one of the shows in this new series, we were supposed to be trapped in a glass shower stall, with the water turned on full blast. The script called for me to dive down and pull out the plug at the bottom of the shower, but when I did this in front of a live audience, I found I had no room to maneuver. I couldn't get back to the surface again. What's more, I had swallowed a lot of water, and was actually drowning, right there in front of three hundred people who were splitting their sides laughing.

Vivian, realizing in cold terror what had happened, never changed expression. She reached down, pulled me safely to the surface by the roots of my hair, and then calmly spoke both sides of our dialogue, putting my lines in the form of questions. Whatta girl! And whatta night!

> *—Lucille Ball recalling the time her friend and costar Vivian Vance saved her life*

If you're ever in a jam,
Here I am.
If you're ever in a mess
SOS
If you ever feel so happy you land in jail
I'm your bail.
It's friendship
Friendship
Just a perfect blendship
When other friendships have been forgot
Ours
Will still be hot.

If you're ever down a well,
Ring my bell.
If you ever catch on fire,
Send a wire.
If you ever lose your teeth when you're out to dine,
Borrow mine.

It's friendship, friendship,
Just a perfect blendship.
When other friendships have ceased to jell,
Ours will still be swell.

—from "Friendship" by Cole Porter,
  from the musical DuBarry Was a Lady

I adored Elsie de Wolfe. She was part of my bringing up. She was a marvelous woman with tremendous taste and a great sense of humor. She was a part of international society, but she never stopped being completely American—a working woman—and she was the most fantastic businesswoman there ever was. . . .

She was a small woman and always perfectly dressed. She started the fashion for short white gloves and for tinting your hair blue, and she knew all about diet and exercise before it was fashionable. She had tremendous chic, which is a word you can't even use today, because there is no chic anymore. . . .

What made her such a success as a businesswoman was her honesty. For all the chic, she was a very sensible woman. You could put her down next to some big shot, and she'd do a deal most men wouldn't pull off in five months. And she did it in a half hour. . . .

Writers and painters live totally private lives, they live inside themselves, but that was not for Elsie. She was not a sit-at-home girl dreaming up houses. She went out into the world, and she loved having people around her. She was greedy, the way people in love are greedy, for more. She loved life, and people, and fun and novelty, and she was never anything but her own self.

—Diana Vreeland on her friend Elsie de Wolfe

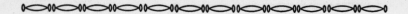

While our two young men were away Katherine and I sat at the fire darning our husbands' socks and talking of our homes and childhood. We conjured up the excitement of the day of a party: the preparations, washing our hair and plaiting it to make it wavy, putting "baby" ribbon in our camisoles; the wonderful feeling of pleasurable anticipation while waiting till the last moment to put on the party dress; then the hooking-up, the few stitches, and the running from room to room to look in the glass; the nice faint smell of the long white kid gloves, the white silk stockings and satin slippers. . . .

I think she found it easy to be with me; we had something in common when we first met, a memory of childhood in a distant provincial setting in another land. It was rather as if we were both exiles and did not quite "belong" in London, but we both loved being alive in this wonderful, beautiful, tortuous, and often torturing world.

> *—Beatrice, Lady Glenavy, Irish painter, on her friendship with*
> *Katherine Mansfield*

In 1945, I was a tall, skinny, shy sixteen-year-old girl from a small river town in Washington State, riding the Los Angeles city bus on Wilshire from Vermont to UCLA in Westwood. I was overwhelmed by the size of the city and attending a college where I knew no one. A cute girl about my age got on the bus at the next stop. Later that day I saw her in a campus bathroom. Feeling out of place and painfully lonely, I introduced myself. She'd been student body secretary at Los Angeles High School and was one of the most popular girls in the freshman class. But, more important, she was very kind, and we became friends.

Both of us had grown up in poor homes with no fathers. We were always broke but shared what we had—food, clothes, apartments, and friends. Beverly majored in Theatre Arts and I majored in Music. After college, Beverly went to New York to be a Broadway star and I stayed in LA, went to work for Joan Crawford, and continued voice training with high hopes for a career in opera. Even though we were on different coasts, we were always in touch. We both married performers; I had four children—one son, three daughters. Bev had one daughter, born the day after my third child. We divorced about the same time, and then remarried years later at about the same time. (She was my matron of honor.)

Beverly is the sister I never had. To this day, fifty-two years later, we see each other as often as possible and still share "the best of times, the worst of times. . . ."

—Betty Marvin, visual artist and writer, on Beverly Dixon Wills,
actress and dialogue director for Murphy Brown

I don't suppose anyone really knows how a creative writer works (he or she least of all, perhaps!) or what sort of nourishment his spirit must have. All I am certain of is this; that it is quite necessary for me to know that there is someone who is deeply devoted to me as a person, and who also has the capacity and the depth of understanding to share, vicariously, the sometimes crushing burden of creative effort, recognizing the heartache, the great weariness of mind and body, the occasional black despair it may involve—someone who cherishes me and what I am trying to create, as well. Last summer, I was feeling, as never before, that there was no one who combined all of that. . . .

The few who understood the creative problem were not people to whom I felt emotionally close; those who loved the non-writer part of me did not, by some strange paradox, understand the writer at all! And then, my dear one, you came into my life! Are you beginning to understand a little better? . . . very early in our correspondence last fall I began to sense that capacity to enter so fully into the intellectual and creative parts of my life as well as to be a dearly loved friend. And day by day all that I sensed in you has been fulfilled, but even more wonderfully than I could have dreamed.

> —*Rachel Carson, environmentalist and writer, on the gift of her friendship with Dorothy Freeman*

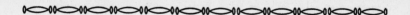

You go on to say—"There is another side to all this—but I can't see that *I* can possibly be giving you anything comparable in return . . ."

If you could go back I think you'd find that my answer was that I was felt in you I had found a kindred spirit—someone who loved and enjoyed the things of the inner being—which I so much needed, for at that time I had no one with whom I could share my deep feelings for music, night, moonlight, sunsets, The Sea (remember) and all the other intangibles which are food for that inner self.

Now 7 years have spun themselves out. And during them you have not only been that kindred spirit in a thousand ways, but you have enriched my life beyond measure.

> *—Dorothy Freeman, describing her friendship with environmentalist*
> *and writer Rachel Carson*

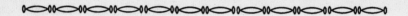

Oona's getting married!!! Carol just called to tell me and I'm so excited. She's going to marry Charlie Chaplin. Imagine! How's Bill, I said, what's happening? Carol is more madly in love than ever with William Saroyan, but he wants her to get pregnant before they get married. I don't get that idea at all, but anyway, that's the way it is. I always thought Carol would get married before Oona, because she caught the bouquet at my wedding, but now it looks like it will be Oona. . . .

Oona and I look alike. We could be sisters. But it's Carol and I who are the sisters, even though we look nothing alike—day and night, you might say. It's funny, though, how connected the three of us are, and all because of Carol. She kind of invents the three of us together, and it works because of this eerie sister look that Oona and I share. But there's nothing invented about Carol and me. From the moment I saw her in the hall that day at Old Westbury Capital I knew we'd be friends for life.

—Gloria Vanderbilt, on her friends Oona O'Neill and Carol Marcus

What does it say about me that my dearest friends in life are all scattered across the globe? That I am drawn to women who, like myself, were either too adventurous or restless to stay in one place?

The answer doesn't matter. I might not see one of my friends for ten years, but when we finally meet, we pick up right where we left off, as if in mid-conversation, and no time has passed at all.

We can talk about anything—no subject is taboo—or we can talk about nothing at all. Her company is enough. It's fun and celebratory, like a box of donuts. She's someone I like to do favors for, who brings out my generous side . . . someone I'm a little bit in love with . . . whom I catch myself imitating because I want so much to be just like her. Yet she allows me to be completely myself. I don't have to worry about being misunderstood. When it comes to knowing who I am, she gets the big picture.

—Gail Lopata Lennon, featured singer with the Lennon Brothers, a forties swing band that performs daily in Branson, Missouri

I've been trying to get Sally Field to wear off-the-shoulder clothes. She has the most beautiful body in the world! I say, "Show your shoulder, it's gorgeous!" and I pull her sweater down. And she says, "Gold, don't ever do that; that's not who I am. You just make me crazy!" And we laugh about it. So guess what? You can't make people be anything other than what they are.

—*Goldie Hawn on trying to change girlfriend Sally Field*

The trouble with the families many of us were born into is that they are too far away. In emergencies we rush across continents to their side, as they do to ours. But our blood kin are often too remote to ease us from our Tuesdays to our Wednesdays. For this we must rely on our families of friends.

These new families may consist of either friends of the road, ascribed by chance, or friends of the heart, achieved by choice. Friends of the road are those we happen to go to school with, work with, or live near. They know where we went last weekend and whether we still have a cold. Just being around gives them a provisional importance in our lives, and us in theirs. If we were to move away, six months or two years will probably erase us from each other's thoughts—unless we have become friends of the heart.

A friend of the heart is one who perceives me as one of the better versions of myself. We make good music, this friend and I, and good silences, too. We phone each other earlier and later than we would dare to bother others. We don't confuse politeness and generosity. At times we argue. We travel together: when cash and time are short, a trip across town will do. Anywhere, just so we can gather, hone and compare our reactions. And, coming and going, we absorb each other's histories.

—*Jane Howard, journalist and author*

Your letters are certainly like drinks of fine cold spring water on a hot day—They have a spark of the kind of fire in them that makes life worthwhile—That nervous energy that makes people like you and I want and go after everything in the world—bump our heads on all the hard walls and scratch our hands on all the briars—but it makes living great—doesn't it—I'm glad I want everything in the world—good and bad—bitter and sweet—I want it all and a lot of it too—Your letter makes me think that life is almost as good to you as it is to me.

> *—Georgia O'Keeffe writing to her friend and fellow painter, Anita Pollitzer (1915)*

Now Pat—Here's why I'm writing.

I saw them yesterday—and they made me *feel*—I swear they did—They have emotion that sing out or holler as the case may be. I'm talking about your pastels—of course. They've all got *feeling* Pat—written in red right over them—no one could possibly get your definite meanings Pat—that is unless they knew you better than I believe anyone does know you—but the mood is there everytime. I'll tell you the ones that I sat longest in front of—

The crazy one—all lines & colors & angles—There is none other like it so you'll know the one I mean—it is so consistently full & confused & crazy that it pleased me tremendously. . . .

   —Anita Pollitzer in a 1915 letter to her friend, painter Georgia
   O'Keeffe (whom she called Pat)

Most of my friends do base, pancake, powder, eye, lipstick, and always keep their nails in perfectly oval shapes with base, color, sealer, and oil for the cuticles. Do I use these things? No. But neither do I put them down and try to make them feel guilty for not being natural. There is something to be said for improvement. I've been known to comment: "Wow, you look really good. Who does your nails?" Why, I even have a dear friend who is a few months younger than I who uses a night cream to guard against wrinkles. Do I laugh and say, "You damned fool, you have no wrinkles"? No, ma'am. I say, "Well, your face is very smooth," which (1) makes her feel good about her efforts and (2) keeps the friendship intact. All of life is a compromise anyway.

—*Nikki Giovanni, poet and author*

Evelyn and I climbed by ourselves for the next few days, choosing our own routes and belaying each other, and as each day drew to an end the realization came into clearer focus. I had learned the basics of climbing and had come to know I was strong enough and agile enough to eventually master the skills. I was surprised and delighted. I'd finally found something I wanted to focus my energy on. Something physical, where I could set goals and achieve things without having to compete with anyone else. Because more than anything, climbing was collaborative.

Learning to climb on the same rope with Evelyn locked our friendship in a much closer bond. She saw the same beauty in the sport, the same potential for personal revelation. With the same commitment, and the same base of physical strength, we worked hard together coaching, helping, and depending on one another for support. Evelyn and I didn't bother with limitations. Looking to the other for inspiration, we went ahead and learned what we needed to know.

> —*Stacy Allison, first American woman to reach the summit of Mt. Everest, on her climbing partner and longtime friend Evelyn Lees*

At long last Emily burst into the room. We were still at an age when girlfriends upon meeting after a long absence did a good deal of shrieking. . . . A bellboy, barely discernible under Emily's mountain of luggage, looked on with disgust until Emily became aware of his presence and with the grand manner of royalty bestowing Maundy money, doled him out a tip. His expression deepened from one of disgust into the epitome of sullen persecution and with a suppressed snarl, he strode from the room. As he turned, I caught a glimpse of the coin Emily had handed him. . . . "Do you never tip more than a penny?"

"A penny? Didn't you just see me give the boy a dollar?"

"No, my dear, I just saw you give the boy a penny."

"Nonsense," she snorted, "I gave him the largest coin I had. What's more, it was an English coin."

"Yes. And it was an English penny. Two cents in America." Grabbing up her purse she rushed from the room crying, "Wait! I didn't mean it!" after the bellboy who by now had vanished past a turn in the corridor. It was some time before she returned. Knowing Emily and knowing she attracts incident as blue serge attracts lint, I grew apprehensive. When finally she returned her face was the color of borscht before they add the sour cream. It seems that after making good with the bellboy, she had wandered back counting her change, opened a door she for some vague reason thought was ours, and had acidly remarked, "Well, I hope you feel better now" to what when she looked up proved to be an elderly gentleman completely nude . . . I assured her this was just one more proof of how broadening travel could be. . . .

—*Cornelia Otis Skinner on going to Europe with her friend Emily Kimbrough*

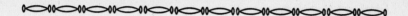

I think Cornelia Otis Skinner works harder than anyone else I know, and I have known her since we were seventeen. From that day, I have, with everyone who has heard or read it, rocked with joy at her humor and her wit, and I am still reduced to the behavior and noise of a loon when I am with her. But even more than these, the qualities at which I marvel are her capacity for work—theatre, writing, and radio—and her precision. . . .

From the day we met, at seventeen, in all the experiences we have shared—although my arrival has been invariably inaccurate and unpunctual—we have laughed, or cried, simultaneously, and always with deeper enjoyment or comfort because the other one was there.

> *—Emily Kimbrough on her friend and coauthor, Cornelia Otis Skinner*

. . . It is much pleasanter to meet Ellen any day than to part with her. When she quits a place she generally leaves an uneasy vacuum behind her, for though not a rattling or dazzling, she is a very acceptable companion. I understand well the feeling you affectionately express, that when you are a little depressed it does you good to look at Ellen and know that she loves you. I am not acquainted with any one whose influence is at once so tranquil and genial as hers. Faults she has because she is human, but I daresay in your pilgrimage through life, you will meet with few whose slight defects are counterbalanced by so many sterling excellencies.

—Charlotte Brontë describing her dear friend Ellen Nussey in a letter to another friend, 1847

I first met Babe shortly before Leland and I were married; Bill had called Leland to invite us out to the country for lunch because he wanted me to meet Barbara. The first meeting proved to be quite a shock. In those days I was very sure of myself. But when we arrived at Kiluna Farm, I took one look at Barbara Paley and thought, "Well, Slim, you're not number one, she is."

I'm not by nature a competitive person. Even if I were, I couldn't help but like Barbara, she was just so marvelous. We eventually became the Paleys' neighbors in Manhasset; from there, Babe became the best woman friend I've ever had. She possessed all the qualities that one looks for in a female friend—totally trustworthy, kind, thoughtful, and funny. I admired her more than any woman I've ever known, on every level. And I learned a tremendous amount from her about character, goodness, kindness, manners— hers were the best of anyone's—and taste. Babe wasn't as smart as my friend Irene Selznick, few people are, and she wasn't as provocative as some other women I've known, but all-round Babe Paley was the *best* woman I've ever known.

—*Slim Keith on her friend Babe Paley*

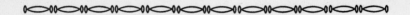

On a night like many others, the phone rings. It is my closest friend and she announces herself simply, "It's me."

She is just starting her own business and I know this week has been packed with meetings.

"How *are* you?" I ask, which in women's shorthand means "How do you *feel?*"

"Eh." Pause. Her meeting, she says, went fine, but she's sitting in her house with clothes strewn everywhere. She doesn't know what the hell she should be doing or where she's going. Should she get a file cabinet or should she clean up her house? As it is, her husband's already bitching and moaning about the sty. Then again, she'd just rather stay in bed. Or go on a vacation. Like three years.

I reassure her. "I got more pleasure from petting my cat today than doing anything else."

We laugh and then get down to business. Together we figure out she's not too terrific about setting priorities. We make mental lists and then devise a game plan: This week write the proposal for the new business; next week clean up the slop and get a file cabinet.

"Well," she says, "how about you?"

—*Eva Margolies on providing "phone therapy" for her best friend*

[Mr. Balanchine's] goddaughter, Kathy, was one of a few friends my age with whom I shared the secrets of growing up. Like every other student in our class, she and I idolized George Balanchine from a distance. As he was a legend and the authority figure within our world, we were naturally in awe of him. Though seldom at the school, he was the stern master of our daily lives, the patriarch of our extended family. His presence was felt by everyone. He oversaw every detail of his productions at the New York City Ballet. He was the one who had choreographed *The Nutcracker*.

Scheming to make a favorable impression, Kathy and I decided to send Mr. B a card. It was a fan letter in the form of a watercolor and poem. As if on a secret mission, we set out one night to deliver our handiwork to his apartment, which was in the same building as my family's, the Apthorp on Upper Broadway. At the time Balanchine lived there with his wife, Tanaquil LeClercq, a former ballerina who had been tragically stricken with polio.

Kathy and I, like a pair of tiny thieves, pushed our card under Mr. B's door and tiptoed away. Our reverence and terror were so great that we dared not disturb his privacy. Nor were we bold enough to sign our names to the card. Our act seemed nothing less than an attempt to communicate with God.

> —*Gelsey Kirkland, ballerina and author, recalling the exploits of two starstruck ten-year-old dancers*

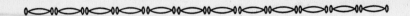

Ava was like my younger sister; she and I were spiritually akin. The main thing is that she was Southern. Though I was born in the East, I was sent South when I was five years old and I lived around the kind of people that she lived around. Ava was not one of those la-di-da Southern ladies. She was of a breed that, when they're wonderful, really are. She didn't feel she was born to rule. She felt that life was crappy and that a lot of people got mistreated for weird reasons, and she liked to see people like each other. She was a real good dame. . . .

We talked about the nonsense about *Show Boat*, the fact that she was going to do it and I wanted it. "I'm sick of these sessions," she'd say. "I don't know how to sing." The reasoning behind it made her angry, for my sake. "Forget it," I said. We knew, we understood why it happened. So there was no friction about it. We were both very logical. It was a big laugh.

If Ava came to you, you couldn't help but like her, because she wasn't competing with anybody. She walked a mile in everybody's shoes. She really did.

—Lena Horne on her friend Ava Gardner

Laurie Kaufman and I did everything together until my family moved across the country the summer before my senior year in high school. The summer after I graduated, I flew back to California and lived with the Kaufmans while Laurie and I worked as counselors at a day camp. We developed a "mutual crush" on Dan, one of the male counselors. The amazing thing was, there was no competition or jealousy involved. It was truly a joint project. One night we invited him over for dinner. We were planning to make our "specialty"—*manicotti con amore*, manicotti with love.

We went to the store and bought all the ingredients (except the meat, which we were going to take from Laurie's freezer). It smelled great while it was cooking and we figured it would be a big hit with Dan—until Laurie looked at the package and realized we had accidentally used the dog's ground meat! We burst into hysterical laughter, rolling around the kitchen floor holding our stomachs until Laurie's mother walked in. (Did we throw it out or decide to serve it anyway? I wish I remembered!)

There are some special friends with whom I have had a deep and intimate connection. We shared fears, hopes, and what was important in our lives. Even when many years have passed between reunions, I have been surprised and moved by the way we instantly experience the same level of intimacy and ease. I feel blessed by such connections and friendships.

—*Melinda Milberg, attorney, on her lifelong friend, Laurie Kaufman, doctoral student*

From Louise I learned that my kneesocks had to match my shetland sweater and that the length of the sweater was crucial—it had to come down over the hips so only six inches of pleated skirt showed. The sleeves were then pushed up midarm. I wore my hair shoulder-length in a pageboy and cut my bangs like hers. To complete the look, I had a single strand of pearls hanging almost to my knees. I bought a trench coat like hers and wrote on it with blue ink. I wrote on my saddle shoes, too—we were walking graffiti. She taught me the useful trick of copying French verb conjugations and Latin declensions on my shoes before a test. If it rained, the ink smeared and I was outfoxed—the ablative and the subjunctive blurred into each other. . . .

Before I met Louise, I was on the outside looking in. I passed the Blue Corner, an ice cream parlor on Jamaica Avenue, and longed to go in and hang out with the crowd, but I was too scared and meek to attempt it until Louise looped her arm through mine and led me in. In no time we left the counter stools and headed for a front booth next to the jukebox, where the seniors sat. Once my foot was in the door, I became a habitué, calling it the "B.C." and chatting with the owners on a first-name basis. But it was really Louise who took all the steps first. . . .

—Anne Jackson, actress, on her friend Louise

It was around this time that old Anney entered my life. I say old Anney, for she has a wit and wisdom way beyond her years, but she was a fat, revoltingly stagestruck twelve-year-old when I first encountered her. She wormed her way into my life with a persistence that makes one wonder how the British lost the Empire. She gave me no choice but to notice her, for wherever I went in England, there she was. With a spy network that would have made the CIA envious, she seemed to know my every move. She'd play truant from school and as if by magic would appear from behind a trunk at Victoria Station, peer through rehearsal studio windows, and once she arrived at Southampton docks in her school uniform with a cake iced "from your little ray of sunshine." By chance, this cake presentation was televised and I felt very guilty when she gleefully told me that her headmistress had seen it and she'd been expelled from school. Anne is one of life's true eccentrics, and that's from one who knows a true eccentric when she sees one. I soon grew to love her dearly and she became my "adopted daughter."

Anney grew up and became my dearest, in fact my only, woman friend. She's now slim, very beautiful, and extremely talented. . . . In 1979 she gave birth to my goddaughter and named her Hermione—poor child! It's only Anney who would choose a godmother who is not religious, hates children, and lives three thousand miles away.

—*Hermione Gingold, actress and raconteuse, on her actress friend,
Anne Clements, Lady Eyre*

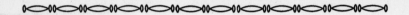

I knew Pat was the one we should hire when she told us about making a special "certificate of achievement" for an assistant who had to retype an entire project at the last moment. Her special human touch was exactly what we wanted as we were building our staff at the Rialto Square Theatre. Who would have known that was the beginning of a sixteen-year friendship? Now my best friend, she shared the same vision for that theatre and "thought big" even though we were in the heart of Illinois and a long way from the big time.

We both met Mark on the same day. He had come in from New York to oversee a production at our newly restored theatre. Our entire department loved him from the beginning. Highly competent, easy to work with, he was sweet and kind, plus he was the only guy we knew who could still fit in his tight Levis and look good. We liked him so much that Pat and I both said if we ever got married again, Mark would be the guy to marry. And so six years later, I did!

—Colleen Wyse, Glamour *magazine beauty director, on her best friend Pat Katisch, marketing consultant*

I always figured some cosmic force brought Colleen into my life. In 1981 I was a single mom just recovering from a devastating divorce when three friends called me within an hour to urge me to apply for a publicist position at the Rialto Square Theatre in Joliet, Illinois. Forty-eight hours later, I was face-to-face with the woman who would change my life. We clicked instantly. Both of us had been teachers, talked fast, walked fast, were infatuated with the arts, and loved all things spectacularly executed with finesse and flair! The spooky part: Colleen was searching for someone who could write like the unknown author of a series of articles she had stashed away in her "samples" file. Ironically—and fatefully—*I* was the author of those articles. It was just like Cinderella and the glass slipper! Needless to say, I got the job.

Although she left three years later to follow her true love Mark to New York City, Colleen has always remained at my side—sometimes in person, and always in spirit—throughout my increasingly challenging career adventures. She has helped me realize dreams I once wouldn't have dared, and she's taught me, "All things are possible." As my lifetime friend, she has embraced all that is good and bad in me, all I've done and all I hope to do—always ready to console, to cheer, to laugh, to encourage, to inspire—and to nudge me past looming doubts and self-constructed obstacles. For all these things, I love her dearly and feel eternally grateful we are the best of friends!

> —*Pat Katisch, marketing consultant, on her friend, Colleen Wyse,*
> Glamour *magazine beauty director*

"Oh, Diana, will you promise faithfully never to forget me, the friend of your youth, no matter what dearer friends may caress thee?"

"Indeed I will," sobbed Diana, "and I'll never have another bosom friend—I don't want to have. I couldn't love anybody as I love you—"

"Oh, Diana," cried Anne, clasping her hands, "do you *love* me?"

"Why, of course I do. Didn't you know that?"

"No." Anne drew a long breath. "I thought you *liked* me of course, but I never hoped you *loved* me. Why, Diana, I didn't think anybody could love me. Nobody ever has loved me since I can remember. Oh, this is wonderful! It's a ray of light which will forever shine on the darkness of a path severed from thee, Diana. Oh, just say it once again."

"I love you devotedly, Anne," said Diana stanchly, "and I always will, you may be sure of that."

—*from* Anne of Green Gables *by L. M. Montgomery*

I am so lucky to have *three* best friends. We love each other and support each other through thick and thin. During my recent divorce, nobody was there for me like Juli, Cali, and Lori. Cali helped me put into words what I was feeling, and during an intensely emotional time, she gave me the strength to face the changes in my life and go on.

We met years ago in high school; we were all new kids who knew nobody, surrounded by cliques that wanted nothing to do with us. So we created our own clique, and ever since we've been best friends. We make each other laugh all the time, and we share a true commitment to friendship.

My three best friends often feel closer to me than any family. They have never judged me, just let me know they will stick by me no matter what. True unconditional love, love that will last a lifetime—I definitely feel blessed!

> —*Laura Sangas, floral designer, on Juli, Cali, and Lori, her sister-friends*

In 1958, the "travel itch" demanded another scratch. This time the ship we took was the *Independence* of the United States Line.

Bette Davis was a fellow passenger. I had never worked with Bette and knew her only well enough to say "Good morning" under the hair dryers in Warner Bros. makeup department.

I was surprised when Bette told me she'd never been to Europe before. She said, "I was sent to London by the studio twice to do pictures, but then flown home immediately to start new ones. When I had the time," she said, "I didn't have the money to travel, and when I finally made enough money, I never could take the time."

Bette was on her way to Madrid to film *John Paul Jones*, in which she would play the Queen of Spain; but this time she hoped to see some of the country when she finished. We were no blasé travelers. We entered the hat contest wearing creations by her sister and my husband, and each of us won a prize. We went down to the economy class, where students and sensible people who save their money travel. We sang for them, which took a lot of nerve, since neither of us was noted for her singing voice. It was made more difficult by the fact that Bette is about five feet two and I am five feet eight, so we couldn't hear each other well enough to stay in the same key, but the audience loved us anyway.

—Eve Arden recalling how she and Bette Davis became friends

I am due to have this friendship with Ethel Waters, because I worked for it.

She came to me across the footlights. Not the artist alone, but the person, and I wanted to know her very much. I was too timid to go backstage and haunt her, so I wrote her letters and she just plain ignored me. But I kept right on. I sensed a great humanness and depth about her; I wanted to know someone like that.

Then Carl Van Vechten gave a dinner for me. A great many celebrities were there. . . . Carl whispered to me that Ethel Waters was coming in later. He was fond of her himself, and he knew I wanted to know her better, so he had persuaded her to come. . . .

We got to talking, Ethel and I, and got on very well. Then I found what I suspected was true. Ethel Waters is a very shy person. It had not been her intention to ignore me. She felt that I belonged to another world and had no need of her. She thought that I had been merely curious. She laughed at her error and said, "And here you were just like me all the time". . . .

Who can know the outer ranges of friendship? I am tempted to say that no one can live without it. It seems to me that trying to live without friends is like milking a bear to get cream for your morning coffee. It is a whole lot of trouble, and then not worth much after you get it.

—*Zora Neale Hurston, writer, on her friendship with singer and actress Ethel Waters*

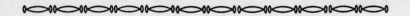

Last winter, left by a beloved boyfriend and in the depths of terrible indecision about work, I flew to Rena's city unannounced, took a taxi to her house, let myself in with my key, and spent the next four days collapsed on her cushy, threadbare sofa, propped up by pillows and wrapped in an afghan, reading a huge Victorian novel and eating cold lasagne from the refrigerator.

Rena would rush out to teach her classes and rush right back to make tea, snuggle in at the other end of the sofa, and then, for hours, just listen to me, commiserating, humoring, reassuring, offering advice.

—Judith Levine, writer, on her friend Rena

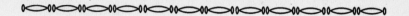

Every May 7, I call my friend Naomi and wish her a happy birthday; every October 1, she does the same to me. We have known each other since we were seven, when our parents thought we should be friends. This year we shall be sixty.

When I hear her voice on the phone, it's as if nothing much has changed since we both lived in suburban London and chased after boys. She had a great sense of mischief. The youngest of three sisters, she couldn't wait to wear makeup and date boys. I was the eldest in my family, and much more serious. When we were 11, she invited me to her birthday party, where there were BOYS and we played kissing games! I invited her to mine, which was only for girls until I was 15. She always asked if she could bring her boyfriend. Naomi has always been lively, cheerful, optimistic, and the person who made me question why I was studying so hard and not having fun.

We drifted apart in our late teens, when I pursued a career, while she became a secretary and enjoyed an active social life. I remember visiting her in the hospital after a serious car accident and making her laugh as I told her about my life as a newspaper reporter.

I married, came to the United States, and had two children, one named David. She married, came to the States, and had two children, one named David. Now she's in California, working for a Unitarian church, and I'm in Colorado self-publishing travel books. She still has that twinkle in her eye, looking round the room for attractive men, while I'm wondering if she's going to suggest something really naughty to do!

—*Evelyn Kaye on her friend Naomi Levitt*

When I was a girl I only had two friends, and they were imaginary. And they would only play with each other.

—*Rita Rudner*

As girls we were literally inseparable. Once we were roller-skating together, and it was time to go home. I skated with her to her house, but we couldn't bear to say good-bye, so we roller-skated together to *my* house. We still couldn't leave each other, so it was back to her house. Finally, one of us—I don't remember which—let the other go home alone. (I still have trouble today taking leave of my friends—sometimes the good-bye takes longer than the visit.)
. . . Mathilde lived in London after the war, and once she came unexpectedly to visit me in New York, when I was to leave for Europe that night. I asked my friend Rudi—unmarried, like Mathilde—to do me a favor: "A friend of mine is here. If you like her, fine. If you don't like her, you did me a favor by showing her New York." They ended up getting married—I am the godmother of their two children.

—*Dr. Ruth Westheimer, author and sex therapist, on her dearest childhood friend Mathilde*

"Lisa," said Ann, "I just want to tell you something. We've known each other too long for this. You can't just disappear. You want to be like Amelia Earhart? You want to be like Judge Crater? You want to be like . . . Barbara? Just slip away forever and hope that after a while it won't matter? Well, it does. I mean, there are always going to be people who float in and out of your life, and you don't see them for years, and then they just show up again. Or sometimes they never show up, and you live the rest of your life without them, wondering what happened, and whatever became of them. Is that what you want? You want to just float away? Well, I won't let you." She paused, but Lisa didn't say anything. "Come on, Lisa," said Ann, "we *know* each other. You can't just disappear; we belong together. Tell me, what else is there in life, what else is as important as your friends? I really want to know."

　　—*from Meg Wolitzer's* Friends for Life

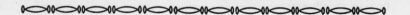

Nona and I were "new girls" in the fall of 1935 at Horace Mann School for Girls in New York City. We developed an almost immediate bond when we discovered we had been born on exactly the same date, September 4, 1919. Only she, a child of Armenian refugees, had been born in Constantinople, and I, in prosaic New Jersey.

Our second bond was author William Saroyan. We both adored him and read and discussed at length everything he wrote as soon as it was published—and he wrote a lot. We spent hours after school walking along Riverside Drive and comparing notes.

Nona was an outgoing, optimistic person in spite of her handicap: She was a hunchback, due to a fall in her childhood. She wore ingenious dresses with sailor collars, lovingly made by her mother, to minimize her hump. A talented writer, she became editor of our school literary magazine, for which I often did the illustrations. She went on to Barnard while I went to Bennington in Vermont.

We kept in touch over the years with newsy Christmas cards. In 1989, I visited her in her office at *The New York Times*, and over lunch we caught up. She'd never married, but was devoted to many nieces and nephews; she was working on a definitive biography of Saroyan and planning a research trip to California. I urged her to visit us there, but she never made it.

She died of a heart attack in spring 1991, and her *Times* obituary filled me with amazement: "literary critic, essayist, and former editor of *The New York Times Book Review* . . ." Was this the same modest and down-to-earth soul mate I had known in high school?

I still miss her every Christmas when her card fails to arrive.

> —*Betty LoMele, artist, recalling her unique best friend, Nona Balakian*

When I am in the company of women . . . I relax about my attractiveness, in the broadest sense of that word. I feel accepted as I really am. I can eat garlic, reveal the fact that I'm wearing torn underwear, commiserate about certain ineptitudes. Most important, I can tell my stories and feel that they are heard and appreciated, because my listener is like me. ("Really??" she will say. "Yes!!" I will answer, happy as a clam.)

—*Elizabeth Berg, writer and editor*

For seventy-two hours Nancy lay in a coma. The doctors said that even if she did come out of it, they had no idea what kind of condition she would be in. For three days I hardly left her side. I talked to her constantly, trying to breathe life into her spirit. I told her that life was worth living—that no matter what troubles come your way, life is a positive thing. I didn't know if she could hear me, but she could. She did. In the end, Nancy says, "God didn't want me and the Devil didn't want me, so they gave me back to Gabe."

And to me. What a bond Nancy and I have. That happened thirty-five years ago, and . . . through all those years, she's breathed life into my spirit time and time again, just the way I did for her in that hospital room.

> —*Virginia Clinton Kelley, mother of President Bill Clinton, on her dear friend Nancy Belinge*

Particular friendships. That was the first time anyone had said that to Anna. PFs, they called them in the convent. From the French *amities particulieres*. Friendships between the same sex. Something to be avoided, abhorred. But no one could think that of her and Lis. It was actually painful to have to say, "It's not . . . a sensual relationship. It's not possessive at all, not exclusive. It won't hurt the community. And I'm a better person because of her." That was true, surely. She felt immense tenderness for Lis, but they never so much as touched. Just that one time, when Lis had put both hands round Anna's face framed in the wimple, and whispered, "Your lovely medieval face." Silently she had put away Lis's hands but she'd wanted to cry: It was recompense for all the years when she had no idea what she looked like. . . .

—*from* Body and Soul *by Marcelle Bernstein*

The one who dies last has to edit the book. That's my pact with Gail. The book is our collected correspondence—up to now, about fifteen years of weekly letters. Hard copies. We figure we'll be an invaluable resource for some twenty-first century graduate student. Meanwhile, we amuse, encourage, and admire ourselves—two poets who met through the pages of a literary magazine where we found each other's work—with a perpetual conversation that could make us immortal. If our poems don't.

> —*Barbara Loots, writer, on her friend, Gail White, poet and medical transcriber*

For Barbara
(on the publication of her poems)

A paradox: paper, quick
to crumple, easy to burn,
perishable as grass,
makes the best wings for a journey.

Adrift in your floating ark,
with all your beasts around you,
send out a paper dove:
it will rescue someone from drowning

perhaps, and return to you
with a branch when the tide falls lower.
And your paper coach will come
to the princess alone in her tower.

Poets can laugh like gods
at the rich, the wise, and the proper.
The wealth of the world weighs light
against our sheaves of paper.

For we turn from weapons to laws
when the useless wars are over,
and the print on a single page
gives the bride to her lover.

—Gail White, in a poem written to her friend, Barbara Loots,
on the publication of their chapbook, Sibyl & Sphinx

It was my first flint drawings that at about this time, late 1932 or early 1933, brought me to the notice of Dr. Gertrude Caton-Thompson, who asked me to draw the stone tools from her famous excavations at Fayoum in Egypt for her book *The Desert Fayoum*. Gertrude was the epitome of that remarkable breed of English ladies who for archaeology's sake would go out alone into harsh desert environments and by determination, skill, expertise and endurance achieve discoveries of major and permanent importance. I immediately liked Gertrude, who had a strong presence but a kind nature and seemed to treat me from the outset as an equal whose professional assistance she was asking as a favour, though as I saw it she was really offering me an extraordinarily attractive opportunity and at the same time showing me an ideal towards which I might aim my career. . . .

It was Gertrude Caton-Thompson who introduced me to Louis. . . .

> —*Mary Leakey, archaeologist, on the friend who would change her life forever*

Whitney is my sister. It is hard for me to remember how famous she is sometimes. But I've told her that I might have to drop her because she is just *too* famous. . . . We talk about everything there is to talk about. She's a down-to-earth person. When we met, it was as though God put her in my life. I love her and we talk about everything. She's a mom now. The show business side of our careers. Family. We treasure each other's friendship.

—*CeCe Winans, gospel singer, on her friend Whitney Houston*

When we first met, it was a spontaneous connection. It was just instant love. . . . I know I can count on CeCe. What's the line in that song? "When I come to you with hurt and truth, I know that you'll stay with me."

—*Whitney Houston on her friendship with gospel singer CeCe Winans*

"Have an eggroll, Mr. Goldstone," Maydee belted out, giving the song from *Gypsy* some Ethel Merman–like gusto as she chased the fifteen-year-old boy around the stage of the junior high auditorium. Her verve, volume, and talent captivated everyone who knew her only as the school attendance clerk. It took nerve as well as talent to be the only adult in the revue my son sang in.

Years later, after a chance meeting in a coffee shop, we realized how many interests we shared. We spent evenings at Maydee's, playing Scrabble, Boggle, Trivial Pursuit. We were both "game people" and I'd been looking for years for someone to match my zeal for playing. We even did puzzles together—jigsaw and crossword—as we listened to show tunes and songs from the '40s.

She was a cancer survivor—ten years; and I was witness to the same kind of nerve she earlier displayed onstage as she went through one false hope after another as symptoms returned. She was a fighter and she would conquer this thing. Courage was her middle name; Maydee, her unusual first name, fit my unusual friend. She'd only finished high school but she was self-educated, well-read, and very intelligent.

Common interests—isn't that what brings friends together? And what cements the friendship but sharing our fears, our hopes, our lives with deepest respect and love. So it was as she sang and joked her way through mounting pain. I saw her every day at the hospital and held her hand until it was time to let go. She did that gracefully, too. Our games had ended, but the memory of Maydee lingers on still.

—*Shirley Sayre, retired teacher, remembering her friend Maydee Esau*

I first learned about women's friendships from my mother. When I was a little girl, my mother spent time with her many friends at our house and sometimes I would sit under the kitchen table pretending to play while I listened to them talk. When I began to grow up and could not fit under the table anymore, sometimes the women let me sit at the table with them and listen, and sometimes join in the conversation.

It seemed to me that those women were conducting the most important business in the world as they talked together and that they were having a whole lot of fun doing it. The warm, reciprocal, nurturing friendship they shared was one of the reasons I wanted to grow up to be a woman.

—*Susan Koppelman, editor and writer, on her lifelong fascination with women's friendships*

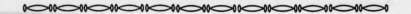

Regardless of where we are in the world, we will either talk or be together on our birthday [April 24]. She is sentimental that way, and we are family.

She is a woman I feel attached to, and I love her and appreciate what she does with her life. She is an inspiration to me because whatever baggage she carries around with her as a Taurus is the baggage I carry myself.

May she shine forever, because then I and others like us can see ourselves.

—Shirley MacLaine on her longtime friend Barbra Streisand

I don't know if I've had a past life, but somehow I feel Gayle and I have been connected before. When I met her, it was as if I met someone who mirrors exactly who I am. We share the same kind of hopes and desires. We get irritated over the same things. It's uncanny, but Gayle and I feel the same way about *everything*. I'm closer to her than anyone else in the world. She is my family. If anything ever happened to Gayle, it would be like losing a part of myself.

—Oprah Winfrey on her best friend Gayle King

We're not related, but I feel like we are kin. With Sisters, you are looking for understanding, sharing in many dimensions, and sharing in confidence. That's the key. You have someone with whom you can vent the frustration of the moment. If you let it out around the wrong people, it could end up being harmful to your career. But when you tell Sister-friends, it goes no further.

—Arnette Hubbard, Chicago election commissioner, on her friendship with attorney Anne Fredd and librarian Geri Thigpen

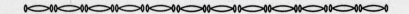

We reverted back to those wonderful days when the biggest decision we had to make was which street to take home. We talked the way we talked when we were eight, with an honesty that would be embarrassing to most people who are casual friends. We can do that because we are not casual friends, thank God. There are too many of those in these times when small towns are becoming extinct and everyone moves from their urban places every seven years. New friends are fine, but this kind of friend is precious. Like good therapists, we know one another's full histories, from the beginning.

—Julie Hatfield on the reunion of her oldest and dearest friends

One of the greatest gifts Rachel gave to me in her life, I received after her death. I designed and sewed a Names Project Quilt panel for her, and in the process, I discovered that I could sew. I even like to sew. In fact, I love to sew. I have begun to make clothing for myself, and with every piece I complete, I thank my friend Rachel. . . .

Rachel's quilt panel reads:

> Rachel's soul is deep and wide, and if she touched your heart, you *knew* it. She could be *so* difficult, and she is so loved. . . .

> —*Judith Black, writer and artist, recalling her friend Rachel Ellyn Hertzberg-Thurman*

"They sent for me, Penelope—of course I never would have dreamed of applying. Even if I'd been smart enough, I never would have applied for *your* place! And I always supposed they thought I was too stupid. You'd tried so often to get me into the schools that I didn't suppose there was any chance for me. When they sent for me, I thought it must be a mistake. I couldn't believe it! And even when I found they really wanted me, I couldn't bear the idea, Penelope. I said if it had only been any other place but yours; but they said that was the only one that was vacant. And of course everybody said you'd never come back here—you were so positive you wouldn't. Penelope—" She paused, shrinking back from the unrevealed mystery of her friend's return. "And I've got so many to think of that it didn't seem as if I ought to refuse. But I said I'd only take it on one condition. I made them solemnly agree to that— that if you changed your mind and—decided to come back to Sailport—"

"I know that, too," said Miss Bent, slowly. Bending forward, she kissed the wet cheek of her friend . . .

—*from "Friends" by Edith Wharton*

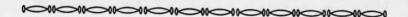

We fight to talk. We have always talked simultaneously, each determined to prevail, for as long as thirty seconds at a time. It is our only competition. I can talk to her endlessly about my children; she never grows weary of it, expects and receives the same indulgence from me. She is as pleased with the turns my life has taken as I am. There is no conflict for her between then and now. It is not that I have not changed, for the changes are many and deep, nor that she does not perceive them, but rather that she is pure love, pure acceptance. She is the friend/mother/sister that we all wish we had; the one who gives us support without diminishing our independence, and who gives us continuity without denying our changes. To be around her is to feel happy.

—*Nancy Eberle, journalist, on a precious friendship*

When we are able to forgive ourselves, we may be able to forgive our friends. And as we find we can trust our friends, we learn to trust ourselves. Confidence and self-confidence interact in complex ways, and as we value other women more highly, we gain a greater esteem for ourselves.

—*Uta West, author and lecturer*

One night I went to see Susan Freundlich sign a Tom Paxton concert. I'd never seen her work from out front but always to my left onstage. She was great. So was Tom. That night, Susan and I sat in the hotel bar and time caught up with us. We had loved each other for years, we had worked close and hard, we had held each other when exhaustion and frustration took over, we had confided in each other about love and sex and fear, we had flirted wildly without hidden intention, we had struggled. . . .

As we sat peacefully together, we wondered out loud why we had never been lovers. Promising that we would not let the root of our friendship be altered, we spent the night together. We kept our promise about the root, but the leaves on the branches changed colors with the seasons. Sometimes we were passionately in love, sometimes we backed away to catch our breaths, sometimes we watched each other fall in love with other people and we made room, noticing our jealousy but not being ruled by it. We work together still.

> —*Holly Near, singer and activist, celebrating her friendship with*
> *Susan Freundlich, sign-language performer and interpreter*

The people from long ago can't be replaced. They carry a part of me with them, and I carry a part of them. In an earlier day, perhaps, when communities were more stable, we would have lived out our lives near each other, and celebrated the birth of one another's grandchildren together. . . .

The people from long ago can't be replaced.

As time passes, they become more important to me, not less. I've learned how precious they are. Staying close to them is like holding hands in the dark.

—*Linda Roberts, columnist*

I met Karen when she was one of a group of prospective creative writing students who visited Washington College my freshman year. I was first drawn to her because of the story she brought to share at the writing workshop. Her skill impressed me and her style seemed a lot like my own. Later I found out that her biggest influence on that story was Ray Bradbury, my favorite writer, whom she also loved. This coincidence turned out to be just one of many as we got to know each other better. We found that we have so many likes, traits, and experiences in common that we've stopped pointing them out in an effort to preserve our own identities.

Often, talking to Karen is like speaking with a wiser version of myself. I regularly play a listening, counseling, "Dear Abby" type of part to many of my other friends. When Karen does this for me, however, I feel like an elementary school teacher going to graduate school. She is truly the wisest, most compassionate friend I have. When I told her I was having a problem with my ex-boyfriend, for instance, she not only gave me advice on how to handle the problem, but also included a long spiel analyzing (extremely accurately) his personal character.

Her wisdom, her caring, and our mutual understanding are what make my friendship with Karen unique among all others. I feel extremely lucky to have met this kindred spirit, and I know that, although we now go to schools two hundred miles apart, we will be very close friends for the rest of our lives.

—*Eva Kaplan-Leiserson, college student, on her friend Karen Kramer*

Eva and I hadn't meant to stay up 'til seven A.M. that first night she came to visit. It was the first time since July that we'd seen each other, and only the second time since I'd left Maryland to return to New York. We had three days, mere moments, really, to catch up on months of inadequate E-mail.

We lay in the dark, we two Dear Abbys, hour ticking after hour, our voices softly murmuring through three A.M. to four.

"Did you see the sky today? It was frosty and gray, the color of pigeons . . . Jimmy Stewart, yes, but only when he's young . . . And Bradbury—I mean, what more is there to say? And Sandra Cisneros, yes, her too . . ."

We fall in love too much, too deeply.

"Eva, please, you can't change him . . . And Karen, please, you shouldn't change him . . . And the sky, Eva, the sky, Karen, wasn't it a glorious sky today?"

In the first light, we birthed a snowy January morning and slept.

Too soon, she departed. "Well, you know," I said. She nodded. "I know."

And I waved from the bottom of the driveway, again at the mercy of Prodigy, of MCI.

But it happens when I see a coral sunset or a cloudy waltz before an autumn thunderstorm. I will a silent wish two hundred miles south, to Maryland, to my sky-watcher who knows: "Look at the sky, Eva. Did you see the sky today?"

And it snows again. It is seven A.M. and it snows.

> —*Karen Kramer, university student, on her friendship with Eva*
> *Kaplan-Leiserson*

Finally I told them about my failed marriage and how I was beginning to blame myself. They wouldn't let me. In fact, they lifted my spirits with funny stories of sweet revenge. . . . Their point wasn't really that I needed to hurl hot grits or make a bonfire out of his tailor-made suits, but that I needed to know how to rise above self-blame . . . how to find, as Toni put it, a place to put my pain. Sometimes something as simple as a haircut can lighten the load, she told me . . . I walked down the street to the barbershop and cut that man right out of my hair.

> *—Pamela Amos-Hooks, freelance TV producer, recalling the advice of her friend, writer Toni Cade Bambara*

She can stay here with me long as she want to. If I eat, she gonna eat. If I sleep, she gonna sleep. If I ain't got nothing but a cotton house, she got a corner . . . we been friends so long—we been together—we just lonesome without one another.

> *—Ruth Scott, 85, on her sixty-year friendship with Hester Hall, 91*

I know that Judy is always there for me. I'm likely to wake up in the middle of the night with an urge to write and feel like driving out to my Tennessee Mountain Home, two hundred miles away. I'll call Judy and ask, "How long would it take you to get ready to go? I'm on a writing binge." She'll be at my door within an hour. Free to go, free to stay, as long as we want or need to. It's a wonderful feeling of freedom to know that you can do a thing like that, with a person who's as excited about it as you are.

Judy will get into my head, waiting eagerly for whatever comes out next. I sit with my guitar, and she writes everything down. Sometimes I'll ask her, "Put down all the words you can think of that rhyme with this or that," or whatever. I tend to forget to eat (if you can believe that) when I'm writing, and Judy always keeps me from hurting myself. Just about the time my blood sugar gets low, she'll be there with a bowl of Jell-O. Writing is an intensely personal thing, best done alone. Being with Judy is better. It's like being alone but with somebody, if that makes sense.

> *—Dolly Parton on her friendship and creative partnership with Judy Ogle*

When we first met nearly twenty years ago, talking got my friend Miche and I into trouble with our boss. We were working in book publishing, our desks one behind the other, and we always had so much fun laughing and talking that our supervisor decided to separate us. She moved Miche's desk around the corner, but she couldn't keep us apart. Even though Miche moved out of New York more than fifteen years ago, we still talk a lot. I refer to her as "word person," the one I call when I'm writing a memo or report and can't think of the word I want. By talking to her and even getting silly about it, I manage to solve my problem.

But our connection runs much deeper. We call each other to gripe, to vent, to talk about whatever's driving us crazy or making us ecstatic, whether it's our husbands, our children, our jobs, or just life in general. What we get from each other is incredible support. And what's unique about Miche is that she focuses on what I'm going through and doesn't filter it through her own experience. I can count on her for an honest response—and a wonderful sense of humor, too. Best of all, I know she's on my side, even when we don't agree. She encourages me to take chances, to make changes, and to keep trying to make sense of it all.

> —*Elizabeth Kurnetz, associate publisher, on her friendship with*
> *Michelle Curry Wright, writer and waiter*

"But don't hold me to that." Liz usually qualifies her outbursts regarding this or that thing, or a him or a her. "I might feel different tomorrow." Throughout the many years of having had such a friend, who gives me the same freedom to change as she requires, I've learned that what is essential is beyond the elbowroom of life—beyond today's fleeting feelings, or hair color change, or newly impassioned self-help doctrine. Beyond it all is handling a friend's heart with care, and helping her feel the crazy singularity of who she is. Everyone should be so lucky.

—*Michelle Curry Wright, writer and waiter, on her friend Elizabeth Kurnetz, associate publisher*

Like most little girls we were very romantic and had our own imaginary boyfriends. We'd make up plays for ourselves and make up stories, and of course I was really *in*, because I could say, "Well, I know Van Johnson, so Van Johnson is going to be *my* boyfriend today. But I'll let you have him tomorrow."

> —*Elizabeth Taylor on how she played with her two childhood best friends, who called themselves The Three Musketeers*

I wish you could know Katherine Loring, she is a most wonderful being. She has all the mere brute superiority which distinguishes man from woman combined with all the distinctively feminine virtues. There is nothing she cannot do from hewing wood & drawing water to driving run-away horses & educating all the women of North America. . . .

> —*Alice James describing her beloved friend and companion Katherine Loring in a letter to another friend, Sara Sedgwick Darwin, August 9, 1879*

Diannia, Melia, Sherry, and I were pretty inseparable in our early years. One time, Diannia and I hid in one of Daddy's trailers so she could spend the night with me. But when Uncle Dale and Aunt Virginia got halfway home, someone missed Diannia and they came back for her. We didn't get into too much trouble for that.

You could usually find the whole gang of us at Sherry's house on a Thursday night, when our favorite show, *Bewitched*, came on. We did fun, silly things together, like read Ouija boards and have séances. Those scared us all to death. We'd get Patty King from across the street because she was the lightest of the group. We'd lay her on the floor, and with two fingers apiece under her, we'd try to raise her off the ground. One time, we did lift her off the floor. We were so frightened when that happened, we dropped her!

—Reba McEntire recalling silly times with childhood best friends

Remember when we used to sit in your father's car when it was parked in the driveway? We packed our dolls in the backseat and we drove clear to California. We chatted and laughed and pointed out the scenery as we followed the highways of our six-year-old imaginations.

And now, so many years later, our roads have converged once again. How grand it is to laugh and share the experiences of all those wide highways, narrow little lanes, detours and dead ends that we each encountered along the way.

No one knows the mysteries of this journey with quite the same understanding, appreciation, or sympathy as you do. So long ago, two little girls took those first steps on the same old road together. . . .

  —Christine Stratton, office manager, on her "on the road" friend,
  Gail Benton Estes

Ali MacGraw was a true-blue friend. We had met my first summer modeling in New York when she worked as a photographer's stylist. Dashing off drawings, collecting accessories, bringing her instinctive sense of style to the set, she radiated intelligence and vitality. Sassy and classy, she could charm a snake if she chose to, and I was drawn to her generous spirit. But it wasn't until years later, when we were both in films and living in Los Angeles, that we became close friends, spending long evenings by the fire at her house at the beach, catching up on changes—or lack of them—in our lives and occasionally weathering rocky reviews together.

—Candice Bergen on her friend Ali MacGraw

I was an eighteen-year-old virgin child. She introduced me to adult life, to a professional life, and to what was to be the best part of my emotional life.

The ties that bound us were those, plus a built-in unexplainable female bond of understanding. She was a beauty with an original mind, and she responded to my mind. I was shaped by her husband to be the celluloid Slim, so we were, of course, inextricably bound. She was irresistible because, among other things, she responded to my humor. And she laughed out loud and completely. And I was oh so glad of that, because I felt she had an enormously sad center. I never mentioned it to her, but I felt it. . . .

When Bogie wanted to buy me a present, his first, she had gone with him to choose it. It was a gold identification bracelet with my name on the outside and "The Whistler" engraved on the inside. So as long as the bracelet and I are together—and we still are—Slim will be part of my life.

> —*Lauren Bacall on the early days of her friendship with Slim Keith, who, as Mrs. Howard Hawks, discovered her for films*

I met Joy in the early 1930s at Hunter College; she was my close friend and schoolmate. In the college yearbook, among the photos of the graduates, all women, all young, all with identical discreet black velvet V-necks and marcelled hair, I see my own photo—how young I was! And here is Joy, with her dark, limpid doe eyes and soft round face, looking grave and lovely. She did not have time to grow old; she died in her forties.

We both went on to Columbia for graduate work, she in seventeenth-, me in eighteenth-century English literature. In those days I was diffident, and what I admired most in Joy was her daring and independence. Though ladylike, cultivated, and soft-spoken, she liked to jolt others by her nonconformity. I remember how shocked we were (This was in 1933!) when she mentioned that she used to go to burlesque shows.

> —*Bel Kaufman, author of* Up the Down Staircase, *remembering her friend, poet Joy Gresham, whose life with C. S. Lewis was described in* Shadowlands

All I can do is be with her. I help Wendy to her bed when she comes home from the mastectomy. I hold her head every other Friday night when she vomits the poisons from her body. I put my arms around her in sessions when she cries and pounds out her rage and her terror. I help her eat the absurd overabundance of soy loaf and banana bread and lentil soup with which her panicked mother continually stuffs her refrigerator. I buy her bright teal cotton socks and slip them onto her icy, twitching feet while she shakes with chemo sickness.

Wendy decides to skip the last two treatments. She tells me her oncologist says it's okay for her to do that. Michael says it's okay with him. It's not okay with me.

I want to drag her to the doctor's office and stick the IV in her arm myself. I want to have a big screaming fight with her about my rights as her best friend, and I want to win the fight. I want to learn to love her on her terms, the way she deserves to be loved. I want her never to have cancer again. *I want her to outlive me.*

    —*Meredith Maran on friendship "in sickness and health"*

A few years ago Cindy and I went to our high school reunion. The sharp crowd saved a seat—one—for her at their table. She didn't take it. She took a seat next to me.

"You didn't have to do that," I said.

"I know," she replied, "but they were then and you are always."

—Nancy Kelton, essayist and teacher, on her friend Cindy

A true friend reaches out before she's asked for help or is even sure she'll be welcome. When I was going through a very hard time a few years ago, I didn't want to talk about it. My friend Madge arrived on my doorstep one day and said, "I just thought you might need a hug." She hugged me and left. I suddenly felt that things weren't quite as bad as I thought.

—Lois Duncan, author and columnist

Just before I left her house about midnight, she said she had something for me. Then she gave me a great big box filled with clothes for me to take home. One thing in that box was a little, red, sexy, shorty nightgown. She told me, "This is the sexiest thing I've ever had. Red is the color men like."

. . . Before we said good-bye, we'd usually hug each other, but that night I was carrying that huge box. Patsy said, "Aren't you going to hug me?" I put down the box and hugged her. Then came the last words I would hear from her. She said, "Little gal, no matter what people say or do, no matter what happens, you and me are gonna stick together."

—Loretta Lynn remembering her friend Patsy Cline

Cali and I traveled to Maui together in 1988. I was at a point where I had to make a major decision about what to do with my life. It was an incredible bonding experience between friends. We did nothing but eat tuna and lounge, just what I really needed. No worries, we promised ourselves, just have fun.

We had a blast, strolling down the main drag of town arm in arm, singing along to Tracy Chapman's "Fast Car" on a Sony Walkman with two sets of earphones. Cali is someone I can totally be myself with. She never judges anyone, she accepts everyone with open arms. We enjoyed every minute together. I came home from that trip with a great attitude, and I made the best decision of my life so far. I couldn't have done it without Cali. She's an incredible listener and a wonderful supporter of being yourself. She always says, "Live, laugh, love—every day of your life!"

I can't imagine what my life would be without her.

—Lori Dinham, mom and barista, on her best friend Cali Turner Alpert

The teacher asked for volunteers to help the new students find their way around. When it was my turn, only one hand went up in all the room.

The hand was attached to Monica. She had lots of brown hair that wouldn't stop curling, and gray eyes with a navy rim, and she wore braces. She looked as exotic to me as I must have looked to her in my secondhand clothes and painfully straightened hair. Monica remembers different things than I do. She recalls thinking it was brave of me to come to a classroom where nobody else was black. She remembers, too, that she was the class loner, an outcast among a small group of children she had known since second grade. She remembers thinking, as she raised her hand, that perhaps she could make a friend.

—Rosemary L. Bray, essayist and editor, recalling how her friend Monica reached out on the first day of school

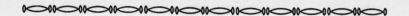

I met my best friend Jean in a film class when she said Alfred Hitchcock was overrated. I disagreed and we argued out of the building and into a lifelong friendship where we argue still. We became friends without meaning to, and took our intimacy step by step. Deliberate choice, not desperate need, moved us closer. Our friendship is so much a part of us now that it seems unavoidable that we should have become friends. But there was nothing inevitable about it. It's easy to imagine Jean saying to me in that classroom, "Hitchcock's a hack, you're a fool, and that's all I have to say." But that was not all she had to say. Which is why we're friends today. We always have more to say.

—*Jennifer Crichton, writer, on agreeing to disagree with her best friend Jean*

In St. Croix with my friend Suzanne . . . I got stuck in a sand trap from which I couldn't extricate one leg, and the blue-green waters of Sue's beach buffeted me. I couldn't at all breathe, slammed by all that lovely liquid this way and that. Caught in seaweed, I was torn between the necessity to relax and the necessity to energize so as to free myself. Suzanne put her strong brown arms around me and with utter unselfconsciousness breathed into my mouth. "Do you suppose," I asked Sue, sitting on her terrace that night, "that life is a matter of swinging from one polar opposite to another and of achieving balance through grace? In this case, through your grace, perhaps through the grace of God—the breath of God?"

"Oh, you silly," she said, and swung her legs over the rail.

—Barbara Grizzuti Harrison on her friend Suzanne

In time we became like a well-functioning family. Fluctuations of mood were treated with exquisite delicacy. People just naturally fell to lowering their voices and tiptoeing about when my migraines struck. We were always prepared to offer hours of sage advice when Mina exploded in the door from the lab, seething about some fresh incident of sexual harassment. Jana's courtship and eventual engagement to Bob Kiely proceeded with the help of a bevy of sympathetic observers ready during the inevitable collisions and missed communications of bridging between Europe and America to translate from new world to old. After the announcement of Jana's engagement we all learned with horror of her denunciation by her thesis director. He had greeted her happy news with white-faced rage, telling her that because she entertained the thought of marriage, she was a frivolous woman who would never make a committed scientist. The attack was chilling, since it underlined all too clearly the terms on which we were participating in a male-controlled academic world. Yet it could not dim the intense pleasure we took in each other's company and the enchantment of sharing a collective life of the mind.

> —*Jill Ker Conway, university president and author, on the Harvard graduate school friendships that sustained her*

When my best friend moved to Salt Lake City we both knew it meant the end of a way of life, of late nights at our favorite bar, long heartfelt phone postmortems, intimate familiarity, fierce loyalty—sisterhood bordering on romance. For a while I was bereft. But life swept on, of course, and forced me to accept the relationship's diminished form, the occasional calls and letters dwindling even more when she married. But here's a funny thing: Whenever we *do* talk now, the old charge blazes again like a gas jet turned up, and we lapse easily into the rhythms of a language we invented over many years.

—Joan Frank, writer

MIMI: You can be close with husbands and children, but a best friend enriches your life in a different way. We've always said we'll still be together when we're old, old ladies in our rocking chairs.

LORRAINE: We're going to laugh all the way to the grave.

—Mimi Meltzer and Lorraine Sloan, best friends and Los Angeles interior design business partners

After Josh, I lost a baby, stillborn. Another little girl. Susan wrote me a letter full of such fiery feeling that it actually made a tiny difference where all else had failed. I have kept it. In the letter she managed what no one else had dared attempt—to speak of Isobel as a real, whole person.

"*I want us to have a wonderful, long lunch, and I want to know all about your youngest daughter* [she wrote]. *I want to know who she looked like, what she weighed, what colour her eyes were, and her hair (if any). I want to know what name you've given her, and all about the godawful funeral service. I wonder if I might be her godmother. I'd make a lousy godmother in real life and I don't have any of the right credentials, but I know I'd be good at thinking about your lost little girl, and talking about her so that she stays in the family. . . .*

Susan's words breached the dam and allowed me to cry.

—*from* Life After Lunch *by Sarah Harrison*

I met Lucy about twenty years ago; she's in her forties now and I'm in my seventies. We liked each other for all kinds of reasons, even if we didn't always agree on ideology. In fact, once we had a really bad, knock-down, drag-out fight and I said to her, "Well, I guess this is the end of a beautiful friendship." She looked at me and said, "No, it's not." She was right, of course. It was too good to let go because we disagreed on an issue or two.

In 1993, I slipped and broke my ankle. Lucy came to the hospital and said, "Don't worry, dear, you'll stay at my house when you get out." When I left, I stayed in her living room for weeks. Then, in 1996, I took a bad flop and broke my hip and arm. I was in the hospital for a month. Lucy came often to visit and told me, "Don't worry, dear, when you get out, you'll come and stay at my house."

But a week before I was released, Lucy was kicked by her horse. She broke a major bone in her leg between her knee and ankle. We got out of the hospital at the same time and had to take care of each other. Because I was in a wheelchair, I did the rolling around and getting of stuff; because she was on crutches, she could stand at the stove and do the cooking.

Lucy and I are both "yang"—forceful, dominant personalities. In fact, our friends placed bets ranging from four days to a week and a half before we couldn't stand it anymore. Well, we made it through the whole thing—and remain the closest of friends.

> —*Blanche Edwards, retired natural-foods shop owner, on her friend Lucy, former Green Party nominee for New Hampshire state office and natural-foods shop manager*

Few comforts are more alluring for a woman than the rich intimate territory of women's talk. . . . A woman friend will say, "You are not alone. I have felt that way, too. This is what happened to me." Home, in other words.

—*Elsa Walsh, reporter*

What would we have done without friends in adolescence to help us navigate the travails of puberty and deal with our "unreasonable" parents? And what about our twentysomething romances? Whom do we go to when in the dating years the man of our dreams becomes the stuff of nightmares? We go to our friends. Later, they coach us through first-time motherhood. Years later as we help our kids pack for college, they witness our tears. Our friends walk with us through menopause as, once again, we are caught up in the hormonal crazies, and they listen as we fantasize about fleeing to the Caribbean or a convent.

In their presence, we laugh about what drove us crazy hours before; with them we cry without shame, knowing we will be understood.

—*Brenda Hunter, psychologist and author*

I hope you will remember to miss me, you know you promised to and I am counting on it. I wish I had it in me to tell you just how grateful I am to you for this winter but I cannot. I think you have the gift of kindness, it seems to come without any effort and without the least trace of fussing. All through these months I am quite sure you have never failed to do the kindest possible thing, the quite unnecessary thing often, and yet you have never made me feel—in spite of my natural suspiciousness—that you were bothering about me a bit.

> —*Alice Hamilton, social reformer, writing to her dear friend and*
> *fellow activist, Katherine Bowditch Codman (1920)*

I write HONORA on the sparkling sand!
    The envious waves forbid the trace to stay:
Honora's name again adorns the strand,
    Again the waters bear their prize away!

So Nature wrote her charms upon thy face—
    The cheek's bright bloom, the lip's envermeilled dye,
And every gay and every witching grace
    That youth's warm hours and beauty's stores supply.

But Time's stern tide, with cold Oblivion's wave,
    Shall soon dissolve each fair, each fading charm;
E'en Nature's self, so powerful, cannot save
    Her own rich gifts from this o'erwhelming harm.

Love and the Muse can boast superior power;
    Indelible the letters they shall frame:
They yield to no inevitable hour,
    But on enduring tablets write thy name.

—*Anne Seward, eighteenth-century poet and beauty known as the "Swan of Lichfield," on her adored friend Honora Sneyd, whom she called, "more lovely, more amiable, more interesting than any thing I ever saw in the female form"*

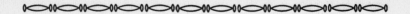

We had faced disintegrating forces over which we had triumphed. Our friendship had survived extraneous influences which at moments could have proved its undoing. We might easily have become victims of misrepresentation and of envy, had our anchorage been less secure.

Whereas, despite all environment and every condition, through fair weather and foul, our craft of mutual faith and mutual affection glided steadily forward, and the friendship between us which was founded upon the rock of sympathy, of love and above all of respect, has withstood the strain of nearly forty years, combining in one the relations of companion and sister. . . .

In all that is external we are as remote from each other as the poles. Yet the water flows on, the tide rises and falls, the waves tower and recede, the undertow sweeps along the driftwood and tosses it upon the beach, while nothing alters the eternal strength of the ocean which is so much greater than the ripples of the river.

Emerson's definition of a friend is "that being before whom one can think aloud."

Was there ever a more sublime interpretation? It means the denuding of one's very soul before that other soul which can understand.

It is not the record of one's sins and of one's virtues but of all that stands back of them. It is the chronicle of what life has meant or can mean to my friend and me. It is a priceless treasure, a gift from God in very fact. It is the song without words which in the singing becomes the ladder of souls stretching from earth to heaven.

—*Bessie Marbury on her devoted friendship with Elsie de Wolfe*

It was as if we'd always known one another. We saw each other every day for the next eleven years. Our friendship was metaphysical, rapturous. We were all things to each other. We were mothers to each other, we were daughters—sometimes we were little girls giggling in the attic, other times we were wise old women talking about our men, our kids. "You're my best friend," she'd say solemnly. We addressed each other as "Grace." "How you doin', Grace?" we'd say, and then we'd laugh uncontrollably. Diane drew the story of my life out of me and we exchanged secrets, ideas, memories. She was never judgmental about me or anybody or anything.

—*Cheech McKensie on her friend, renowned photographer Diane Arbus*

I met my sister/friend Vicki at a retreat in Philadelphia in 1995. I was a senior at Union Theological Seminary and I needed a thesis break. Vicki led a Bible study. I connected with her spirit immediately. Somehow she was the child in me that needed healing. We exchanged telephone numbers and addresses. Since the day we met, we have been communicating and loving each other. She lives in Delaware and is a student at Harvard. Sometimes I feel her despair, and I call her, and she will always say, "I was just thinking about you." Or I will be needing a friend and she will call me, and I will say, "How did you know?"

I love Vicki. We will be friends and sisters forever.

—Reverend Margret Marie Powell, chaplain at Momentum AIDS Project, on her friendship with Reverend Vicki Lyn Tuck, pastoral counselor

"And who is the princess?" I would ask. "You are," Gwladys would answer. "You have long golden hair down to your knees and deep-blue eyes, and the fairest white skin with pink cheeks. And you have a chaplet of wildflowers on your head...."

"And who are you?" I demanded, already knowing the answer.

"A witch," said Gwladys, "a dreadful, terrible old witch with one tooth like a Chinese sword, eyes like burning coals and long black snakes for hair and fingernails three feet long with a different poison in each nail." I shuddered and was almost afraid to raise my eyes, because I knew that Gwladys was turning herself into the witch at that very moment. From being a meek, furtive little girl, she became a thing of terror and menace....

My role as the peaches-and-cream princess was that of the fly caught in the spider's web. I had my beauty and my fine garments and eventually my prince (because Gwladys was fair-minded), but I certainly had to suffer for it. Up and down the stairs of the castle, running ever faster and faster, ducking behind a tapestry, crawling under a silken table cover, or even hanging from a battlement—it was to no avail. Gwladys always caught up with me ... It was only toward the end of the afternoon, when teatime was approaching, that she would allow the prince finally to do her in....

With the other children I knew I played the games that children have always played. But hide and seek and spoon-and-egg race and pinning the tail on the donkey, under the supervision of a kindly governess, were pretty dull when compared to the breathtaking, mad afternoons with Gwladys.

> —*Brooke Astor, philanthropist and author, on her adored (and sometimes terrifying) friend Gwladys*

July 21, 1995
Glenno's Pizza in Scott County, Route 35 South, Minnesota

Stacie and I are in a restaurant from which the customers had fled hours ago, not knowing whether our car will be still be outside once we decide it's safe to leave. We recall the events of the last hour with some amusement:

The colors surrounding us were illuminated by the strangest streams of light as we left St. Paul, and of course we didn't think twice about heading toward the darkest part in order to get to our next destination. As I confidently drove into the blackness, cars were leaving the interstate and the local weather station started listing counties toward which tornadoes were heading! Our reaction was typical—relaxed exhilaration rather than the more appropriate fear. Stacie checked the map and assured me that we were nowhere near the announced Scott County. "It's much further north than we are, so don't worry, we'll be fine. Let's listen to some music." Suddenly sheets of water came violently crashing down on the windshield at the moment I deciphered the "Welcome to Scott County" sign outside Stacie's window. Only then I remembered how sketchy my dear friend's navigation skills were: "You could have told me you were reading the map upside down!" She replied, "Rebecca, there must be two Scott Counties!" After this amicable outburst, and before being whisked up into the sky, we promptly exited the interstate.

It is moments like this that always remind me of my innocent faith in Stacie and the precious and tacit trust we have in one another.

> *—Rebecca Boyle, artist manager, on her friend and navigator,*
> *architecture student Stacie Wong*

21 July 1995, 10:45 P.M.

Typical of our luck, we have found ourselves amidst tornado warnings with only a Chrysler Neon as shelter. Rebecca is driving assuredly in the pelting rain under a pitch-black sky. I am attempting to hide my poor map-reading skills dismally aided by a dim flashlight. A radio news flash soon interrupts: "Blackness overtakes the sky ... funnel cloud movement unpredictable ... roads extremely dangerous ... avoid the counties of Marengo, Scott ..." Rebecca calmly inquires, "Are we anywhere near those counties?" I reply a confident "No" as I frantically scan the road atlas. Suddenly, a "Welcome to Scott County" sign zooms past our windshield with perfect comic timing in a not-so-funny situation. Our prospects are not good. Visions of hydroplaning and being sucked away flash through my mind. Instead, with a little drama and a great deal of divine intervention, we find a lone pizza joint and receive the comforts of hot coffee, a curious waitress, and David Letterman on the television ...

We could have died that night, but the experience is memorable for a different reason. Rebecca's good-natured ribbing at my lack of direction made me appreciate the way we understand, support, and challenge each other. Everything intellectually, emotionally, and day-to-day is fair game as ammunition for humor and heated debate. At the end of the day, however, nothing is held against you. You sleep and prepare for another day of kinship and spontaneous sparring, and wait for the next mishap that is inevitably around the corner.

> —*Stacie Wong, architecture student, on her friend, artist manager*
> *Rebecca Boyle*

Elizabeth leaves in an hour. It has been a good visit, and I wish she lived nearby, for again I take strength and joy in the friendship of someone older than I. It is a rest to be with someone who has made her peace with life and enjoys everything so much. I am keenly interested in the young women who come here with their fervors, their problems, their hopes, who come to me, I suppose, to reaffirm a vision of life or a way of living that appeals to them. But they cannot know what such a life costs. They take so much for granted, and when I look back at myself at twenty-five or thirty, I am newly aware that so did I. Youth is a kind of genius in itself and knows it. Old age is often expected to recognize that genius and forget its own, so much subtler and gentler, so much wiser. But it is possible to keep the genius of youth into old age, the curiosity, the intense interest in everything from a bird to a book to a dog that I have witnessed these past days in Elizabeth Roget.

—*May Sarton, poet, on the special pleasures of older friends*

Oh, if I could just get my arms around you!—And stay with you like that for hours, telling you so many things, & listening to all that you must have to say.—I love you very much, dear Anne, & I always shall.—Ours was a perfect friendship—I knew it at the time—and it is still just as true. I would do anything in the world for you, & I know that you would for me.—And it doesn't matter if we never write, and never see each other, it is just the same,— except that it would be so nice to see each other!

—*Edna St. Vincent Millay in a letter to her college friend, Anne Gardner Lynch*

This strange, lovely, furtive creature never has seemed to me to be made of common flesh and blood. She was rather like some Diana of the realm of the mind who, though she had forsaken forest and the chase of deer, now treads the ways of man still carrying hidden under her veil her crescent of light. She comes and goes, she folds her cloak around her and vanishes, having shot into her victim's heart a quiverful of teasing arrows. . . .

To this visitant from another sphere our lives appear more strange, more vivid and fantastically exciting than they do to oneself.

As years have gone by, and her sojourning here has inured her to our ordinary life, she seems now to sit with almost familiar ease in my room, and I no longer feel the fear that this enchanting and bewildering goddess will sail away before I have recovered from her entry and before I had caught a glimpse of her crescent light. I feel I have made her see into my heart.

—Lady Ottoline Morrell on her friendship with Virginia Woolf

To M.J.

Dear Jim:

This book is your fault. If it had not been for your brutal insistence, Lord Peter would never have staggered through to the end of this enquiry. Pray consider that he thanks you with his accustomed suavity.

Yours ever,
D.L.S.

> —Dorothy L. Sayers, *dedicating her first book,* Whose Body? *(which introduced Lord Peter Wimsey), to her close friend Muriel Jaeger, (nicknamed Jim)*

"I hope you'll let me write something for the book, a little preface or something, anything." She'd said it as if the decision would be mine, if I deigned to let her do it, if I would bestow upon her the honor of allowing her to contribute to my book.

If you play your cards right, Mary Frances, maybe I'll let you get a word in edgewise. But don't count on it. That's what I should have said. But instead I looked down at the floor and nodded and mumbled. It wasn't eloquent, but what it meant was, "Thank you, Mary Frances. Nothing would make me happier, nothing could be more just than to have one page of you bound in with all those pages of me, as if we were throwing a party together. After all, it's your fault that I'm in this position; it was reading your books way before I met you that got me to think of food as something more than overdone roast lamb, to think of life as something more than overdone roast lamb . . ."

"Thanks" was all I actually managed to say, but for the rest, well, I thought she knew.

> —*Jeannette Ferrary on her friendship with renowned food writer*
> *M.F.K. Fisher*

Growing up, my best friend and I were like Frick and Frack; she was like my shadow. She's in a wheelchair now—she was in a car accident. So I feel a great loss from that. But as I get older, I know she's still my friend, and more than anyone she's teaching me about my life. Every friendship is a circle and you have all these circles stacked on top of each other, all turning . . .

What I mean is, friends come and go and you move on. There are people I went to school with who I've lost touch with, but I know they're still my friends . . .

[Emerson] talks about how friends are like books—you know where to find them but you don't use them all the time. He's right. Sometimes you just need to know where your friends are.

> —*Parker Posey, actress and award winner at Sundance Film*
> *Festival, 1997*

I need you more and more, and the great world grows wider, and dear ones fewer and fewer, every day that you stay away—I miss my biggest heart; my own goes wandering round, and calls for Susie—Friends are too dear to sunder, Oh they are far too few, and how soon they will go away where you and I cannot find them, *don't* let us forget these things, for their remembrance *now* will save us many an anguish when it is *too late* to love them!

> —*Emily Dickinson writing to her beloved friend Susan Gilbert, 11 June 1852*

Endowed with the warmest and most grateful of human hearts, she united to the utmost delicacy and nobleness of sentiment, active benevolence, which knew no limit but the furthest extent of her ability and a boundless enthusiasm for the good and fair, wherever she discovered them . . . Of envy and jealousy there was not a trace in her composition; her probity, veracity, and honor were perfect. Though as free from pride as from vanity, her sense of independence was such, that no one could fix upon her the slightest obligation capable of lowering her in any eyes. She had a generous propensity to seek those most, who needed her offices of friendship. No one was more scrupulously just to the characters and performances of others, no one more candid, no one more deserving of every kind of reliance. It is gratifying to reflect to how many hearts her unassisted merit found its way.

> —*Lucy Aikin describing her dear friend Miss Benger, nineteenth-century English writer*

I'm really lucky, I have a core group of friends, and I have invested a lot of time in them and in their lives. And no matter what happens, they will always be there for me. Because, let me tell you, I need my friends. I need them all the time. It's not just a matter of when you're feeling down. I need my friends as a constant reminder of the goodness of human relationships. It's a very reassuring and wonderful thing to know that there is a group of people who care as much about you as they care about themselves.

—*Ann Richards, former governor of Texas*

Now I am fourteen! The noise is finished, the celebration is over and everything is calm once again. But I am trying to improve my disposition and I have taken sweet Eleanor, my best friend, as my model, because in her I find all the qualities that I lack. When I am with her, I feel a great longing to become good. When her beautiful blue eyes look at me and plunge into my soul, I earnestly want to be able to look at people as directly as that, for her eyes hide nothing. In her gaze, one can read her mind like an open book, and I love to read it because of its beauty.

> —*Anaïs Nin, novelist and diarist, on the dear friend of her youth, Eleanor Flynn*

Saralee, one of my oldest friends (with whom I shared a gym locker in college, and double dates; whose maid of honor I was, in a purple dress she made for me herself), smiles a lot, sometimes a kind of abashed grin at her silliness, her fears, sometimes because so much amuses her. She talks effusively, a good storyteller, and asks a thousand questions, gives forth a thousand answers to questions you haven't asked. . . .

It has always been, for Saralee, as if every fact or event or action has equal weight, or maybe none at all, and thus deserves to live in the public domain. She has no secrets, and doesn't much understand why other people do. I sometimes think, though I'm not notably reticent, that she makes me more modest than I'd ordinarily be, as if I were putting on scarves in the presence of a nudist. Sometimes I turn away blushing from the direct blast of her questioning.

—*Rosellen Brown,"The Uncertainty Principle"*

I met Deb, one of my two closest friends, in kindergarten. My sister also babysat for her and her sisters, and I would sometimes tag along. Then her family moved into the house across the street, and soon we were spending all our time together.

During the summer, we were inseparable, and always found something to do. Once, we created our own balance beam on the front yard with my father's sawhorses and a long 2 x 4. We spent hours working on elaborate routines, both individually and as a team. The finale of our team routine called for us to place our hands on each other's shoulders, balancing on one foot. After a third bounce, we would jump in the air simultaneously and land on the beam together. We counted, we jumped, and then one long 2 x 4 made a loud crack. We landed on the ground, apart from each other, in silence. Once we had both asked, "Are you okay?" and found out we were both still in one piece, we rolled on the ground in laughter. We then hid the broken 2 x 4 under my porch so that my father wouldn't know what we'd done to his lumber. We still laugh about it.

Deb is an important part of who I am today, even if we haven't always been in touch over the years. Friendship can't be measured with time. Close friends are always friends, no matter where you are in your life. The one constant is that you will always be there for her, and she for you.

—*Nicole Trider, homemaker, on her friend Debra Schott, marketing manager*

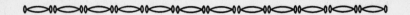

I very soon took to going to her for advice, for reaffirmation and for critical help. Although she never admitted to the role, although we worked in alien styles, she became a kind of mentor. After every concert I rushed to her for analyses. Three times she said the word that has picked me up, dusted me off, and sent me marching, the word that has kept me from quitting.

Why could one believe her? Was it the sense of obsession in the face, or the sheer integrity of her life? One faced a woman who for better or worse never compromised, who, although she had known prolonged and bitter poverty, could not be bought or pushed or cajoled into toying with her principles. She was a brave and gallant creature. . . .

Martha Graham moved like an angel in the night. Just to know she was there finding paths where my feet trod vapor, was companionship. "We all go through this," said Martha. "You are being tempered. You are a sword in the fire."

—*Agnes de Mille on her friendship with Martha Graham*

On the first day after the clinic that Abby and I spent together I told her that meeting her was going to change my whole life. She seemed neither threatened nor surprised by this information; if anything, she was mildly pleased. "Life gives us what we need when we need it," she said. "Receiving what it gives us is a whole other thing."

. . . I said to Thomas, "I have a met a woman who, if she were a man, I would be in love with." But of course Abby could have never been a man, and I fell in love anyway. It's not the kind of definition Abby would have gotten mired in, but I think she may also have been a little in love with me.

Once, on the phone, when we weren't sure if the conversation was over, when we weren't sure if we had actually said goodbye, we both held our receivers, breathing silently, till finally she had the guts to say, "Are you still there?"

"We are a couple of silly women," she said, when we had finally stopped laughing. "A couple of silly women who want so badly to be friends."

—*Pam Houston, "In My Next Life"*

Mary is a diabetic and, as a result, watches her diet carefully. While the rest of us were chowing down, she used to use the lunch break to do what she liked best. A mirror would be rolled in onstage, along with a piano and a piano player (he walked in). Soon, several of Mary's dance-class buddies would arrive, along with her dance teacher. They would have an hour dance class every day, which was a delight to watch. Then the dancers would scatter, and Mary would have a quick shower, and something very light to eat as we went back to the afternoon's rehearsal.

This was all *very* noble, but once in a great while, Mary's halo would slip. She'd get a gleam in her eye around eleven o'clock in the morning, look at me, and say, "What are we doing for lunch?" That meant it was binge day.

When lunchtime rolled around, we would head for Art's Delicatessen. Sometimes one or two of the others would join us, but usually it was just the two of us sinners. We would indulge in humungous sandwiches and French fries. Mary would even start it off with a bowl of borscht—my chance to be noble. But wait—on the way back to the studio we would hit Baskin-Robbins for double-decker ice cream cones! . . .

(Let me hasten to add that this happened very rarely and long ago. Mary devotes so much of her time, energy, and money to the Juvenile Diabetes Foundation that the above was only an aberration; we knew it was wrong.)

> —*Betty White on that true mark of friendship: sharing a rare eating binge with Mary Tyler Moore*

In the circle of her private friends, as well as from her own heart, she learns what constitutes the happiness and the misery of woman, what is her weakness and what her need, what her bane and what her blessing. She learns to comprehend the deep mystery of that electric chain of feeling which ever vibrates through the heart of woman, and which man, with all his philosophy, can never understand.

> —*Mrs. Sarah Ellis (1845) on the power and uniqueness of women's friendships*

If I think of the woman I admire and love the most, it would be Beverly. She has taken the deepest tragedies in her life and withstood them and even embraced them with love. She is not a saint. She can be funny, gossipy, and tough in the best sense of the word.

And I am very influenced by Beverly. She and I are in similar stages in our lives, not wanting to give up our careers, but feeling that it's time to enjoy our lives and those we love.

> —*Barbara Walters on her friend Beverly Sills*

Judy and I became best friends in seventh grade at the Albany Academy for Girls. We wore the same pinecone green uniform, but Judy always looked better in hers—this girl had curves before anyone else did. I remember us consuming tons of Bob's Fish Fry and Luigi's Pizza while watching *The Mary Tyler Moore Show* week after week, dimly aware, on some level, that we were a little bit like Mary and Rhoda. Judy was actually a *lot* like Mary—tall, thin, attractive, and *completely* emotional. She would cry over *everything*— and I don't mean simply the tearjerker scenes in movies.

We got together for our twentieth high-school reunion three years ago, which was a little disappointing since so few Academy Girls showed up. But the pre-reunion "sleepover" at Judy's house— without husbands and children—was the *best*. We had a license to be teenage girls all over again.

These days we mostly keep in touch by E-mail. Only a few days ago, Judy warned me (about as breathlessly as E-mail can get) that the latest copy of our Albany Academy for Girls Alumni Bulletin was erroneously reporting Judy as divorced from a man to whom she had never been married. I joked that maybe I could represent her in her invasion-of-privacy lawsuit—after all, what are (lawyer) friends for? And so we may begin plotting to write the perfect claim letter to our alma mater—the ultimate revenge for all those years of mindless English class writing assignments!

> —*Sara Goodman, attorney, entrepreneur, and mom, on her best friend Judy Serling, writer and mom*

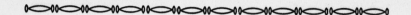

With regard to the choice of friends, there is little to say; for a friend is never chosen. A secret sympathy, the attraction of a thousand nameless qualities, a charm in the expression of the countenance, even in the voice or manner, a similarity of circumstances,—these are the things that begin attachment.

—*Anna Letitia Barbauld, nineteenth-century writer and editor*

"Shirley, I never had a sister—you never had a sister; but it flashes on me at this moment how sisters feel towards each other. Affection twined with their life, which no shocks of feeling can uproot, which little quarrels only trample an instant that it may spring more freshly when the pressure is removed; affection that no passion can ultimately outrival, with which even love itself cannot do more than compete in force and truth . . ."

—*from* Shirley *by Charlotte Brontë*

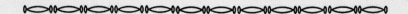

Dian was the most uncompromising person I've ever known in my life, and the most dedicated. But the stories that she was a hermit and didn't like people are a complete fabrication. She loved her friends, and there were a lot of us . . . To her friends Dian was generous to the point of absurdity. She had a genius for finding things. She would go home for a three-week lecture tour and come back with things I'd never seen in America before. Brand-new fantastic things. She did that for everybody.

—*Rosamond Carr on her friend Dian Fossey*

Dearest Mary—

God knows why I write only today. I wrote you countless letters—thanking you, missing you so much, thinking of you with a
new closeness and tenderness. The trouble is that in order to write
you must stop thinking; also, thinking can be done so comfortably,
writing is so troublesome. Forgive me. But think that in the morning we have your divine jelly, the best I ever ate, for breakfast, and
in the evening we drink your wine. And in between, I read (or did
anyhow) the mss. you corrected for me. How are you supposed to
write to somebody who is always around?

> —*Hannah Arendt, political philosopher, in a letter to her dear friend*
> *Mary McCarthy, novelist and essayist*

I thought I could sprinkle water on a drooping plant and it would grow as big and beautiful as it once had been. I didn't know then what all my sleuthing has taught me: that friendship comes with no guarantees and offers no promise of permanence. The happiness wrought from being breath-close and finger-tight is vulnerable. Friends do drift apart because of stolen boyfriends, borrowed shoes returned with scuff marks and hot words—for all those reasons and many more. The bonds that hold people together are not made of steel—they're made of love.

—*Bebe Moore Campbell*

Sisterhood means that if you happen to be in Burma and I happen to be in San Diego and I'm married to someone who is very jealous and you're married to someone who is very possessive, if you call me in the night, I have to come. Whatever I have to pay, I *have* to be there.

—*Maya Angelou*

Sources List

Aikin, Lucy, from *The Friendship of Women* (1868), Roberts Brothers

Allison, Dorothy, *Two or Three Things I Know for Sure*, NAL-Dutton

Allison, Stacy, *Beyond the Limits: A Woman's Triumph on Everest*, Little, Brown and Company

Amos-Hooks, Pamela, *Essence*, May 1996

Angelou, Maya, *Ebony*, July 1990

Ann-Margret, *Ann-Margret: My Story*, G. P. Putnam's Sons

Arden, Eve, *Three Phases of Eve*, St. Martin's Press

Arendt, Hannah, *Between Friends: The Correspondence*, Harcourt Brace & Company

Aston-Nielsen, Taylor, original

Astor, Brooke, *Patchwork Child*, Random House, Inc.

Austen, Jane, *Northanger Abbey*

Bacall, Lauren, *Now*, Alfred A. Knopf, Inc.

Ball, Lucille, *Love, Lucy*, G. P. Putnam's Sons

Barbauld, Anne Letitia, *Dear Friend*, Peter Pauper Press

Beatrice, Lady Glenavy, *Today We Will Only Gossip*, Constable, London

Beatts, Anne, *Vogue*, August 1981

Berg, Elizabeth, *New Woman*, August 1991

Bergen, Candice, *Knock Wood*, Linden Press/Simon & Schuster

Bernikow, Louise, *Among Friends*, Harmony Books

Bernstein, Aline, *An Actor's Daughter*, Alfred A. Knopf, Inc.

Bernstein, Marcelle, *Body and Soul*, St. Martin's Press

Bishop, Elizabeth, "Efforts of Affection: A Memoir of Marianne Moore," *The Collected Prose*, Farrar, Straus, and Giroux

Black, Judith, "Life Is Not Fair," *A Loving Testimony*, Crossing Press

Blattspieler, Terri, original

Bombeck, Erma, *Good Housekeeping*, March 1975

Boyle, Rebecca, original

Bray, Rosemary L., *Redbook*, September 1992

Brontë, Charlotte, *Charlotte Brontë and her "Dearest Nell,"* Smith Settle

Brontë, Charlotte, *Shirley*, quoted in *Woman to Woman* by Tess Cosslett, The Harvester Press Ltd.

Brontë, Emily, "Love and Friendship," *The Complete Poems*, Columbia University Press

Brothers, Dr. Joyce, *Best Friends*, Continuum

Brown, Antoinette, *Friends and Sisters*, University of Illinois Press

Brown, Rosellen, "The Uncertainty Principle," *Southwest Review*, Spring 1994

Brownrigg, Sylvia, "Like Cutting Off My Arm," *Surface Tension*, Touchstone

Burnett, Carol, *One More Time*, Random House, Inc.

Campbell, Bebe Moore, *Essence*, February 1979

Canfield, Katharine, original

Carr, Rosamond, *The Dark Romance of Dian Fossey*, Simon & Schuster

Carson, Rachel, *Always, Rachel*, Beacon Press

Christie, Agatha, *Agatha Christie: An Autobiography*, Collins, London

Comden, Betty, *Off Stage*, Simon & Schuster

Conway, Jill Ker, *True North*, Alfred A. Knopf, Inc.

Crichton, Jennifer, *Ms./Campus Times*, October 1985

De Mille, Agnes, *Dance to the Piper*, Columbus Books

de Beauvoir, Simone, *Memoirs of a Dutiful Daughter*, Harper and Row

DeBerry, Virginia, and Grant, Donna, *Tryin' to Sleep in the Bed You Made*, St. Martin's Press

Dickinson, Emily, *Emily Dickinson: Selected Letters*, The Belknap Press of Harvard University Press

Dinham, Lori, original

Duncan, Lois, *Woman's Day*, February 21, 1995

Eberle, Nancy, *Glamour*, July 1978

Edwards, Blanche, original

Ellerbee, Linda, *New Choices*, February 1995

Ellis, Sarah, *The Daughters of England: Their Social Duties and Domestic Habits*, Charles Griffin (1845)

Ephron, Nora, *Us*, February 1997

Ferrary, Jeannette, *Between Friends: M.F.K. Fisher and Me*, The Atlantic Monthly Press

Fields, Annie, *Memories of a Hostess*, The Atlantic Monthly Press

Flagg, Fannie, *Fried Green Tomatoes at the Whistle Stop Cafe*, Random House

Forster, Suzanne, original

Frank, Joan, *Utne Reader*, September/October 1993

Freeman, Dorothy, *Always, Rachel*, Beacon Press

Gingold, Hermione, *How to Grow Old Disgracefully*, St. Martin's Press

Giovanni, Nikki, "My Own Style," *Sacred Cows—and Other Edibles*, William Morrow and Company

Goodman, Sara, original

Gordon, Mary, *Redbook*, July 1979

Guggenheim, Peggy, *Out of This Century*, Universe Books

Hamilton, Alice, *Alice: A Life in Letters*, Harvard University Press

Harrison, Barbara Grizzuti, *An Accidental Autobiography*, Houghton Mifflin Company

Harrison, Sarah, *Life After Lunch*, Hodder and Stoughton

Haskell, Molly, quoted in *Among Friends* by Letty Pogrebin, McGraw-Hill

Hatfield, Julie, *The Boston Globe*, January 24, 1996

Hawn, Goldie, *Ladies Home Journal*, September 1996

Hellman, Lillian, *Pentimento*, Little, Brown and Company

Hepburn, Katharine, *Memories* by Ethel Barrymore, Harper & Brothers

Holland, Sharon, *Glamour*, November 1990

Horne, Lena, *Ava: My Story*, Bantam Books

Houston, Pam, "In My Next Life," *Cowboys Are My Weakness*, W. W. Norton & Co., Inc.

Houston, Whitney, *Ebony*, June 1996

Howard, Jane, *Families*, Simon & Schuster

Hubbard, Arnette, *Ebony*, June 1996

Hunter, Brenda, *In the Company of Women*, Multnomah Books

Hurston, Zora Neale, *Dust Tracks on a Road*, Lippincott

Jackson, Anne, *Early Stages*, Little, Brown and Company

Jaffe, Evelyn Jacob, original

James, Alice, *The James: A Family Narrative* by R.W.B. Lewis, HarperCollins Publishers Inc.

James, Henry, *The Bostonians*

Jewett, Sarah Orne, *The Atlantic*, May 1875

Johnson, Carol Ann, original

Johnson, Susan, original

Kaplan-Leiserson, Eva, original

Katisch, Pat, original

Kaufman, Bel, *Commonweal*, March 25, 1994

Kaye, Evelyn, original

Keith, Slim, *Slim: Memories of a Rich and Imperfect Life*, Simon & Schuster

Kelley, Virginia Clinton, *Leading with My Heart*, Simon & Schuster, Inc.

Kelton, Nancy, *Parents*, March 1993

Kimbrough, Emily, *Our Hearts Were Young and Gay*, Dodd, Mead, and Company

Kirkland, Gelsey, *Dancing on My Grave*, Doubleday

Koppelman, Susan, *Women's Friendships*, University of Oklahoma Press

Kramer, Karen, original

Kreps, Bonnie, *Subversive Thoughts, Authentic Passions*, Harper and Row

Kurnetz, Elizabeth, original

Larsen, Lyn, original

Leakey, Mary, *Disclosing the Past*, Doubleday & Company, Inc.

Lennon, Gail Lopata, original

Levine, Judith, *Mademoiselle*, April 1984

LoMele, Betty, original

Loots, Barbara, original

Louis-Dreyfus, Julia, *New Woman*, February 1994

Lynn, Loretta, *Coal Miner's Daughter*, Henry Regnery Company

Mackie, Lisa, original

MacLaine, Shirley, *My Lucky Stars*, Bantam Books

Mansfield, Katherine, *Adam International Review*

Maran, Meredith, *What It's Like to Live Now*, Bantam Books

Marbury, Bessie, *My Crystal Ball*, Boni and Liveright

Margolies, Eva, *The Best of Friends, The Worst of Enemies*, The Dial Press

Marvin, Betty, original

McEntire, Reba, *Reba: My Story*, Bantam Books

McKensie, Cheech, *Diane Arbus: A Biography*, Alfred A. Knopf, Inc.

McNamara, Mary, *Mademoiselle*, November 1992

Mead, Margaret, *Blackberry Winter*, William Morrow and Company

Meltzer, Mimi, and Lorraine Sloan, *Los Angeles Magazine*, November 1990

Midler, Bette, *Bette: An Intimate Biography of Bette Midler*, Birch Lane Press

Milberg, Melinda, original

Millay, Edna St. Vincent, *Letters of Edna St. Vincent Millay*, Harper & Brothers, Publishers

Mitford, Mary Russell, *My Garden*, Sidgwick & Jackson

Mithers, Carol Lynn, *Mademoiselle*, August 1980

Montgomery, L. M., *Anne of Green Gables*, Bantam Books

Morrell, Lady Ottoline, *Memoirs of Lady Ottoline Morrell*, Alfred A. Knopf, Inc.

Musher, Amy, original

Near, Holly, *Fire in the Rain . . . Singer in the Storm*, William Morrow and Company, Inc.

Newman, Nel, original

Nin, Anaïs, *Linotte: The Early Diary of Anaïs Nin*, Harcourt Brace & Company

O'Donnell, Rosie, *Us*, June 1996

O'Keeffe, Georgia, *Lovingly, Georgia*, Simon & Schuster/Touchstone

Parton, Dolly, *Dolly: My Life and Other Unfinished Business*, HarperCollins Publishers, Inc.

Perry, Lilla Cabot, *Dear Friend*, Peter Pauper Press

Phillips, Jayne Anne, "Road Trip: The Real Thing," *Between Friends*, Houghton Mifflin Company

Pollitzer, Anita, *Lovingly, Georgia*, Simon & Schuster/Touchstone

Porter, Connie, *Glamour*, April 1994

Posey, Parker, *Interview*, February 1995

Potter, Nancy, original

Powell, Reverend Margret Marie, original

Raphael, Bette-Jane, *Glamour*, September 1994

Reed, Leslie, original

Richards, Ann, *Interview*, February 1995

Roberts, Katharine, original

Roberts, Linda, *Chicago Tribune*, January 3, 1993

Rudner, Rita, *Naked Beneath My Clothes*, Viking

Sackville-West, Vita, "Lighting the Cave" by L. A. DeSalvo, *Signs*, Winter 1982

Sangas, Laura, original

Sarton, May, *At Seventy: A Journal*, W. W. Norton & Company

Sayers, Dorothy, *The Letters of Dorothy Sayers*, St. Martin's Press

Sayre, Shirley, original

Schultz, Valerie, *Commonweal*, May 17, 1996

Scott, Marion, original

Scott, Ruth, quoted by Gloria Naylor in *Essence*, May 1985

Seward, Anna, from *The Friendship of Women* (1868), Roberts Brothers

Shakespeare, William, *As You Like It*, Bantam Books edition

Shure, Jill, original

Sills, Ilomay, *One More Time*, Random House, Inc.

Skinner, Cornelia Otis, *Our Hearts Were Young and Gay*, Dodd, Mead, and Company

Spruill, Nancy, original

Stanton, Elizabeth Cady, "A Feminist Friendship," *The Feminist Papers*, Bantam Books, Inc.

Stoddard, Alexandra, *Living Beautifully Together*, Doubleday

Stratton, Christine, original

Taylor, Elizabeth, *An Informal Memoir*, Harper & Row

Thatcher, Margaret, quoted in *The Best of Friends, The Worst of Enemies*, The Dial Press

Totenberg, Nina, quoted by Lois Wyse, *Good Housekeeping*, January 1995

Toth, Susan Allen, *Blooming: A Small-Town Girlhood*, Little, Brown and Company

Trider, Nicole, original

Vanderbilt, Gloria, *Black Knight, White Knight*, Alfred A. Knopf, Inc.

Vecsey, Marianne, original

von Beltz, Heidi, *My Soul Purpose*, Random House

Vreeland, Diana, *Elsie de Wolfe: A Life in the High Style* by J. S. Smith, Atheneum

Walsh, Elsa, quoted in *In the Company of Women* by Brenda Hunter, Multnomah Books

Walters, Barbara, *Ladies' Home Journal*, July 1983

Wasserstein, Wendy, "The Ties That Wound," *Between Friends*, Houghton Mifflin Company

West, Uta, *If Love Is the Answer, What Is the Question?*, McGraw-Hill

Westheimer, Dr. Ruth, *All in a Lifetime*, Warner Books, Inc.

Wharton, Edith, "Friends," *Youth's Companion* (1900)

White, Betty, *Here We Go Again*, Scribner

White, Gail, *Sibyl & Sphinx*

Wilkens, Laurie, *Yankee*, September 1990

Williams, Akosua, original

Williams, Irene, original

Winans, CeCe, *Ebony*, June 1996

Winfrey, Oprah, *Redbook*, October 1989

Wolitzer, Meg, *Friends for Life*, Crown Publishers, Inc.

Wong, Stacie, original

Woolf, Virginia, *Mrs. Dalloway*, Harcourt Brace, Jovanovich, Inc.

Wright, Michelle Curry, original

Wyse, Colleen, original

Wyse, Lois, *Women Make the Best Friends*, Simon & Schuster

Author's Note

The seventeenth-century sage Balthasar Gracian beautifully expressed the passion behind the creation of this book when he wrote, "Have friends. It is a second life. Remember, we have either to live with friends or with enemies, therefore try daily to make a friend . . . Be not too fragile in bumping against the world, and least so with your friends; for some crack with the greatest of ease, showing that they are made of poor stuff. Such trifles bruise them that real hurt is not necessary. So search out those who promise to last. . . . For knowing how to keep friends is more than knowing how to make them. True friendship doubles the good and divides the bad. It is the only defense against misfortune, and the very balm of the spirit."

For "doubling the good" in so many ways, I want to thank my editor, Denise Silvestro, whose enthusiasm for this subject is never-ending, and her assistant, Martha Bushko, for all her help; my agent, Meg Ruley, whose friendship is as precious to me as her business sense; my parents, who encouraged me and helped me locate some of the most moving stories of real-life friendship; and the wonderful women who opened their hearts and lives to me.

About the Author

Barbara Alpert is the author of *No Friend Like a Sister* and the co-author of seven other titles, including *How to Be a Christmas Angel* (with Scott Matthews) and *Cooking Healthy with a Man in Mind* (with JoAnna M. Lund). A former executive editor with Bantam Books whose articles have appeared in *Cosmopolitan* and *ParentSource* magazines, she teaches book editing as an adjunct associate professor at Hofstra University.